The MAILBOX

The Education Center

SONGS & RHYMES on Parade

grade **PreK**

Ages 3–5

Over 175 upbeat opportunities to improve your preschoolers'

- **Language Development**
- **Early Literacy Skills**
- **Math Concepts**
- **Creative Expression**
- **Plus lots more!**

Turn to page 143 for an easy-to-scan index!

Managing Editors: Lynn Drolet, Sharon Murphy

Editorial Team: Becky S. Andrews, Kimberley Bruck, Debra Liverman, Diane Badden, Thad H. McLaurin, Kimberly Brugger-Murphy, Jenny Chapman, Brenda Miner, Karen A. Brudnak, Juli Docimo Blair, Hope Rodgers, Dorothy C. McKinney, Randi Austin, Pamela Ballingall, Janet Boyce, Marie E. Cecchini, LeeAnn Collins, Patti Curtis, Colleen Dabney, Roxanne LaBell Dearman, Sue Fleischmann, Deborah Garmon, Ada Goren, Cynthia Holcomb, Robin Johnson, Angie Kutzer, Carrie Maly, Coramarie Marinan, Beth Marquardt, Robin McClay, Cara Munch, Keely Peasner, Deborah J. Ryan, Betty Silkunas, Barb Stefaniuk, Leanne Stratton Swinson

Production Team: Lori Z. Henry, Pam Crane, Rebecca Saunders, Chris Curry, Sarah Foreman, Theresa Lewis Goode, Greg D. Rieves, Eliseo De Jesus Santos II, Barry Slate, Donna K. Teal, Zane Williard, Tazmen Carlisle, Kathy Coop, Marsha Heim, Lynette Dickerson, Mark Rainey

www.themailbox.com

Manufactured in the United States
10 9 8 7 6 5 4 3 2 1

D1361264

Table of Contents

Ask me to sing for you!

I learned a

new song today!

I learned a

new song today!

Ask me to sing for you!

Note to the teacher: Copy the brag tags on colorful construction paper. Then have youngsters wear them home to invite questions about a song they've enjoyed singing.

Fall

Signs of Fall
(sung to the tune of "He's Got the Whole World in His Hands")

We [see leaves a-changing] in the fall.
We [see leaves a-changing] in the fall.
We [see leaves a-changing] in the fall.
Isn't fall a beautiful time?

Sing additional verses, replacing the underlined phrase with phrases such as *feel cooler weather, pick juicy apples, pick orange pumpkins,* and *make jack-o'-lanterns.*

I Love My Grandparents
(sung to the tune of "This Old Man")

I love them;
They love me.
They're as nice as they can be.
My grandparents give me lots of hugs each day.
They're the best in every way.

Try this:
● Invite each youngster to hold up a photograph of his grandparents or other special older friends while singing the song.

● Give each student a copy of the song lyrics (page 22). Help her use a stamp pad to make fingerprint hearts next to the top two lines. Next, she glues the song to a larger sheet of construction paper and then gives it to her special loved one(s).

Out in the Orchard

(sung to the tune of "Up on the Housetop")

Out in the orchard, apples grow.
Lots of changes seem so slow.
Look for some flowers; they smell so sweet.
The trees are making an apple treat.
Grow, grow, grow,
New apples grow.
Grow, grow, grow,
New apples grow.
Out in the orchard—yum, yum, yum—
Apples are growing for everyone.

Try this:

● Invite youngsters to settle in for a read-aloud of *The Apple Pie Tree* by Zoe Hall. Students are sure to enjoy the beautiful illustrations that show how apples grow on trees.

● Post a copy of the tree cards from page 23. Use the illustrations to discuss the seasonal changes of an apple tree. Then, as you lead little ones in singing the song, point to each card during the corresponding lines.

Tasty Apples

(sung to the tune of "Bingo")

I like apples, red and sweet.
Apples are delicious.
A-P-P-L-E,
A-P-P-L-E,
A-P-P-L-E,
Apples are red and crunchy.

Try this:

● Write the word *apple* in large letters on chart paper. Glue an apple cutout (pattern on page 22) to a craft stick and use it to point to each corresponding letter during the third, fourth, and fifth lines of the song.

● Show youngsters a different motion for each letter in *apple.* Consider motions such as the following: pat legs for *a,* pat tummy for *p* (twice), pat shoulders for *l,* and reach arms up high for *e.* Then have little ones perform the corresponding motion as they sing each letter of the word.

Leaves Are Falling

(sung to the tune of "Are You Sleeping?")

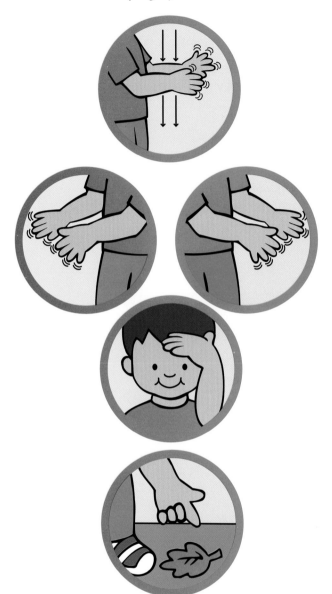

Leaves are falling.

Leaves are falling

All around,

All around.

I can see a(n) [red] leaf.

I can see a(n) [red] leaf

On the ground,

On the ground.

Sing additional verses, substituting a different color word each time.

Try this:
- Cut out a class supply of fall-colored leaves (pattern on page 24). Give each student a leaf and have him drop it when his color is called.

- Sing new verses by changing the underlined word to another descriptive word, such as *big* (stretch out arms) or *small* (cup hands).

- Encourage students to drift along like falling leaves during the song.

Raking Leaves

(sung to the tune of
"I've Been Working on the Railroad")

I've been raking up the fall leaves.
Leaves are everywhere!
Yellow, red, and pretty orange leaves,
Yes, I see them everywhere!
So I rake them in a pile
On this nice fall day.
Whoosh! Here comes the windy weather
And blows them all away!

Try this:

- Share a leaf-related picture book with the group, such as *Fall Leaves Fall!* by Zoe Hall or *Leaf Man* by Lois Ehlert.

- Scatter an assortment of leaf cutouts (pattern on page 24). As you lead youngsters in singing the song, encourage a small group to rake the leaves into a large pile. During the last two lines of the song, use a fan to simulate the wind and scatter the leaves for a new round of raking and singing!

A Busy Squirrel

(sung to the tune of "The Itsy-Bitsy Spider")

The busy little squirrel
Went scampering on the grass.
He found some nuts
And had to make them last.
He dug some little holes
And buried nuts to store.
Then the busy little squirrel
Went out to find some more!

Little Squirrel
(sung to the tune of "I'm a Little Teapot")

There's a little squirrel up in a tree.
I see him looking right at me.
He will run in circles all around,
Then hide his acorns in the ground.

Try this:
- After several singings, give each youngster a brown pom-pom (acorn). Encourage him to scamper around the room pretending to hide his acorn like the squirrel in the song. Later in the day, challenge each youngster to find his hidden acorn—just as a squirrel would.

Gathering Nuts
(sung to the tune of "Head and Shoulders")

Squirrels can hide nuts in a tree, in a tree.
Squirrels can hide nuts in a tree, in a tree.
In the fall they gather lots of nuts.
Squirrels can hide nuts in a tree, in a tree.

Try this:
- Glue a green paper treetop shape to the top of a cardboard tube to resemble a tree. Scatter brown pom-poms (nuts) around the room. Have half of the class pretend to be squirrels hunting for nuts while the other half sings the song. When a youngster finds a nut, he scurries to the tree and puts the nut in the tree. Once all the nuts have been found, have students switch roles and play again.

The Owl Song

(sung to the tune of "Shoo Fly")

Hoo! Hoo!
What did I hear?
Hoo! Hoo!
What was that sound?
Hoo! Hoo!
What did I hear?
Why, it's an owl, loud and clear!

Try this:

● During the first singing, pause briefly after the question in the sixth line for youngsters to share their responses.

● Designate half of the class to pretend to be owls and "hoo" during the corresponding lines of the song. Have the remaining students respond accordingly. After several rounds, invite youngsters to trade roles and sing again!

● For a fun variation of the song, invite a youngster to close her eyes. Then have a different student sing, "Hoo! Hoo! Guess who I am. Hoo! Hoo! What is my name?" When the student is named, select a new volunteer to begin another round.

Sleeping Owls

(sung to the tune of "Are You Sleeping?")

Owls are sleeping,
Owls are sleeping
All day long,
All day long.
They wake up in the nighttime.
For them it is the right time.
Hoot! Hoot! Hoot!
Hoot! Hoot! Hoot!

I'm a Little Firefighter
(sung to the tune of "I'm a Little Teapot")

I'm a little firefighter, don't you know?
Here is my ladder; up I will go.
When I see a fire, I will shout,
"Look out! I'm here to put the fire out!"

Try this:
- Give each student a badge cutout (pattern on page 22) to wear. Have youngsters point to their badges as they sing the first line of the song.

- Encourage little ones to cup their hands around their mouths and shout the last line of the song.

- Discuss with students why a firefighter might need a ladder. Lead youngsters to conclude that a ladder can be used to help rescue people and animals in many different situations.

The Firefighter
(sung to the tune of "My Bonnie Lies Over the Ocean")

The firefighter rides on a fire truck.
The firefighter wears a red hat.
The firefighter carries a long hose
And puts out the fire like that!

Try this:
- Have youngsters pretend to spray a fire hose during the last line.

The Fire Truck's Coming!

(sung to the tune of "The Wheels on the Bus")

The fire truck's coming. Watch out now!
Watch out now! Watch out now!
The fire truck's coming. Watch out now,
All through the town.

Continue with these lines:
The wheels on the truck go fast, fast, fast.
The siren on the truck goes woo, woo, woo.
The lights on the truck go flash, flash, flash.
The people in the town say, "Help, help, help!"
The hose on the truck goes whoosh, whoosh, whoosh.
The flames in the fire sizzle out, sizzle out, sizzle out.
The people in the town say, "Thanks, thanks, thanks."

Try this:

● Color and cut out a copy of the rescue cards on pages 25 and 26. Then use the cards to cue youngsters for each song verse.

● Have youngsters use the rescue cards (pages 25 and 26) to help them transform the song into a class story.

● After singing several rounds, post each rescue card (pages 25 and 26) in a different area of the classroom. Have a few students stand by each card. Then lead each group in singing its verse.

Bye-Bye Crows
(sung to the tune of "The Itsy-Bitsy Spider")

The scarecrow stands out in
The cornfield every day,
Hoping he can scare
Those silly crows away.
When the breezes blow,
He flaps his arms around
And scares those silly crows
Away without a sound.

Try this:
- Try this twist on the game Duck, Duck, Goose. With the children seated in a circle, have a youngster "fly" around them cawing like a crow while you lead the seated students in singing the song. At the song's end, have the crow gently tap the student in front of him and say, "Scarecrow!" Then have the scarecrow chase the crow to the empty seat in the circle.

Mr. Scarecrow
(sung to the tune of "Clementine")

Mr. Scarecrow, Mr. Scarecrow,
In the cornfield looking fine,
Chase away those hungry crows, please,
And protect that corn of mine!

Try this:
- Have each youngster brush an ear of corn with yellow paint and press the painted corn on a sheet of paper to make corn prints. Then have her sponge-paint a green husk on the side of each ear of corn. Display the corn around a scarecrow cutout and lead youngsters in singing the song.

- Have each student color a scarecrow cutout (pattern on page 27) and glue it to a craft stick. Have him use the resulting puppet as a prop while singing the song.

Scarecrow Action Poem

Out on the hill where the corn grows tall,

I see a scarecrow that is made of straw.

When the wind blows, his arms will wiggle

And then his little legs start to jiggle.

He scares away all the crows on the hill,

And when the wind stops, he holds very still.

Try this:
- Have a small group of youngsters stand in front of the class and act out the poem. Invite the remaining students to make the sound of the wind during the third line until it stops in the last line.

- Write the song on chart paper. Then tape a scarecrow cutout (pattern on page 27) to a ruler and use it as a pointer to guide youngsters' chanting of the words.

Silly Pumpkin Patch

One silly pumpkin is big and round.
One silly pumpkin rolls on the ground.

One silly pumpkin is small and fat.
One silly pumpkin wears a silly hat.

One silly pumpkin is thin and tall.
One silly pumpkin shouts, "Happy fall!"

Try this:

- Assemble student copies of the booklet on pages 28 and 29. Have each student complete her booklet by writing her name and coloring the illustrations. Then help her use her booklet as a prop to "read" the rhyme.

- During circle time, pass a pumpkin around the circle while chanting the poem. After several rounds, stop at the end of the second, fourth, and sixth lines for the child holding the pumpkin to say the rhyming word or phrase.

Spiffy Spiders
(sung to the tune of "Shoo Fly")

Spiders are really neat!
Their webs just can't be beat!
They have eight fancy feet.
Bugs and flies are what they eat!

Spooky Spider

Up climbs the spider to his web so high.
There he waits until you walk by.
Down he comes until he's in your sight.
Then, "Boo!" he scares you on Halloween night!

Try this:
- Write the poem on chart paper. Use craft supplies to make a simple spider pointer. Then use the pointer to guide students' reading of the poem.

- Have students compare the spider in the nursery rhyme "Little Miss Muffet" to the spider in this poem.

Costume Choices

(sung to the tune of "The More We Get Together")

What will you be on Halloween,
Halloween, Halloween?
What will you be on Halloween?
Oh, what will you be:
A pirate, a cat,
Or a pumpkin orange and fat?
What will you be on Halloween?
Oh, what will you be?

Try this:
- At the end of the song, invite little ones to share what costumes they will wear on Halloween.

Trick-or-Treat

(sung to the tune of the refrain from "Jingle Bells")

Halloween!
Halloween!
Let us go trick-or-treat!
Grab a bag and take a friend;
You've dressed up oh so neat.
Halloween!
Halloween!
Let us go trick-or-treat!
Remember to say, "Thank you!"
For all your yummy sweets!

Ghosts and Goblins

(sung to the tune of "Clementine")

Halloween, Halloween,
Halloween is almost here.
You'll see monsters, ghosts, and goblins
At this spooky time of year.

Halloween, Halloween,
It is all just make-believe.
And when Halloween is over
All those spooky creatures leave!

Halloween Time

Ghosts say, "Boo!"
Jack-o'-lanterns shine.
Bats fly low.
It's Halloween time.

Cats meow.
Skeletons jiggle.
But they can't scare me—
I just giggle.

Try this:
● Invite one volunteer to be the giggler for the last line. Then divide the class into small groups and assign each group a part in the rhyme. Have youngsters act out their corresponding parts during a reading of the poem.

A Special Day

(sung to the tune of the refrain from "Jingle Bells")

Cook the bird.
Bake the pies.
Oh, so much to do!
Thanksgiving is a special day
For friends and family too!

Try this:
● Ask youngsters to name foods they eat on Thanksgiving Day. Then change the first two lines of the song to match their responses. Examples might include *cook the rice, stir the beans, bake the bread,* and *slice the cake.*

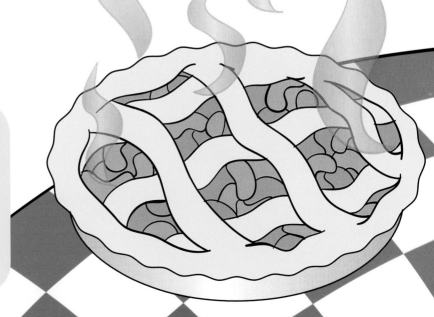

Thanksgiving Foods

(sung to the tune of "She'll Be Comin' Round the Mountain")

On Thanksgiving we eat lots of tasty foods!
Yum! Yum!
On Thanksgiving we eat lots of tasty foods!
Yum! Yum!
We eat turkey, beans, and stuffin'.
We eat cranberries and muffins.
On Thanksgiving we eat lots of tasty foods!
Yum! Yum!

Try this:
- Have youngsters rub their tummies as they sing, "Yum! Yum!"

- Invite students to name their favorite Thanksgiving foods. If desired, record their responses to create a class graph.

Thanksgiving Thank-You

(sung to the tune of "My Bonnie Lies Over the Ocean")

What holiday comes in November
When turkey is what we all eat?
What day reminds us to be thankful?
Thanksgiving, oh yes, what a treat!
Thank you. Thank you.
Thanksgiving Day is here, is here.
Thank you. Thank you.
It's the day we give thanks every year.

I'm So Thankful
(sung to the tune of "London Bridge")

Thanksgiving is almost here, almost here, almost here.
Thanksgiving is almost here.
I'm so thankful!

I'm thankful for the [friends I have, friends I have,
  friends I have].
I'm thankful for the [friends I have].
I'm so thankful!

Sing additional verses, replacing the underlined phrase with phrases such as *food I eat*, *clothes I wear*, and *love I get*.

Try this:
● Ask youngsters what they are thankful for and form their responses into phrases that fit the song.

My Turkey

My turkey has five feathers.
They wiggle to and fro.
My turkey struts and gobbles
Wherever he may go.

Try this:
● Have each youngster wear a simple turkey headband and strut around the room as he recites the poem aloud.

● Invite each student to hold five construction paper feathers and pretend that she is the turkey in the poem. After the last line, have her drop one feather. Then, changing the first line accordingly, lead a rereading of the poem. Continue in this manner until there are no more feathers.

Time to Hide!

(sung to the tune of "Where Is Thumbkin?")

Where's Tom Turkey?
Where's Tim Turkey?

Here I am!
Here I am!

Thanksgiving Day is coming!
It's best if we start running!

Far away!
Hide away!

Try this:
● Encourage little ones to give suggestions for places where the turkeys could hide.

It's a Fall Parade!

Plan a fall-themed parade with your youngsters! Have students make the props and accessories below. Then teach them the provided song and let the marching begin!

Props and Accessories

Fall Leaf Headbands: Have each youngster glue fall leaf cutouts to a strip of construction paper. When the glue is dry, staple the strip to fit the child's head.

Pleasing Pumpkin Mask: Cut facial features in an orange disposable plate for each child. Have each youngster glue a green paper stem and curling-ribbon vines to the plate. Then attach a jumbo craft stick handle to the project.

Glorious Gobbler Headbands: Staple a construction paper strip to fit each child's head. Have each youngster glue facial-feature cutouts to the front of her headband so it resembles a turkey. Then encourage her to glue construction paper feather cutouts to the back of the headband.

Creative Corn: Have each youngster paint a piece of Bubble Wrap cushioning material with several fall colors; then have her place a piece of paper over the wrap and press down to make a print. When the paint is dry, cut a corn cob shape from the paper. Then have each youngster add a fringe-cut piece of a brown paper bag to make a husk.

The Fall Parade Song

(sung to the tune of "When Johnny Comes Marching Home")

What season has leaves of red and brown? It's fall! It's fall!
And great grinning pumpkins can be found. It's fall! It's fall!
There's turkey dinner and corn to eat.
Oh yes, this season is such a treat!
And we all wear sweaters. Fall is the best! Hooray!

Apple Pattern
Use with "Tasty Apples" on page 5.

Badge Pattern
Use with "I'm a Little Firefighter" on page 10.

Grandparents Song
Use with "I Love My Grandparents" on page 4.

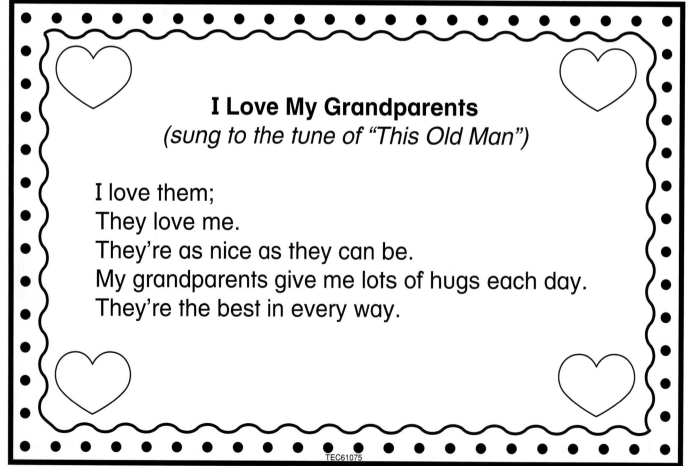

I Love My Grandparents
(sung to the tune of "This Old Man")

I love them;
They love me.
They're as nice as they can be.
My grandparents give me lots of hugs each day.
They're the best in every way.

winter

TEC61075

spring

TEC61075

summer

TEC61075

fall

TEC61075

Leaf Pattern
Use with "Leaves Are Falling" on page 6 and "Raking Leaves" on page 7.

TEC61075

24

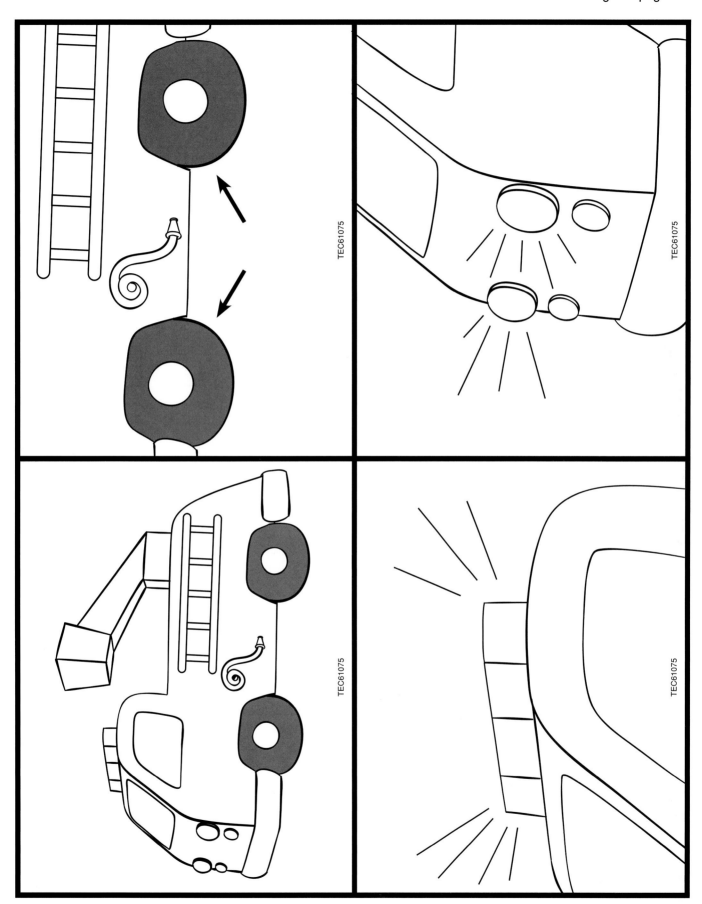

Rescue Cards

Use with "The Fire Truck's Coming!" on page 11.

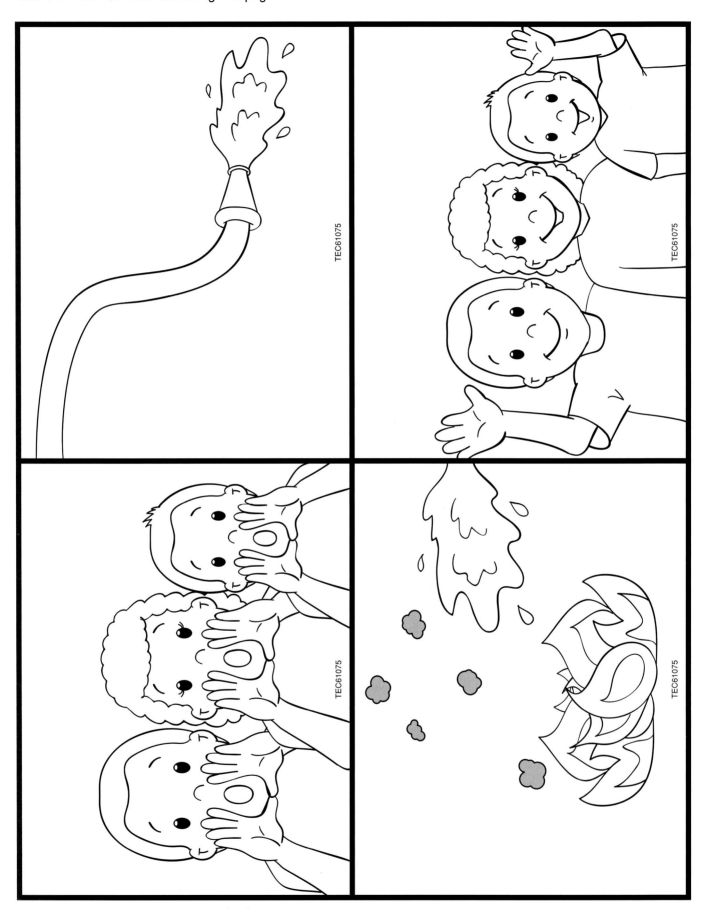

Scarecrow Pattern

Use with "Mr. Scarecrow" on page 12 and "Scarecrow Action Poem" on page 13.

TEC61075

Silly Pumpkin Patch

_____
name

©The Mailbox® • _Songs & Rhymes on Parade_ • TEC61075

One silly pumpkin
is big and round.

1

One silly pumpkin
rolls on the ground.

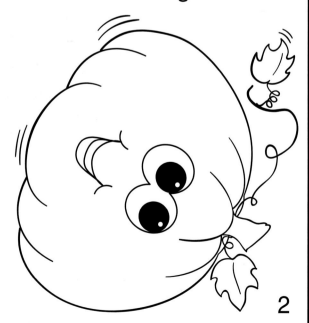

2

One silly pumpkin
is small and fat.

3

One silly pumpkin
wears a silly hat.

4

One silly pumpkin
is thin and tall.

5

One silly pumpkin
shouts,

6

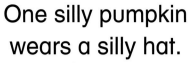

"Happy fall!"

7

Winter

Winter Is Coming
(sung to the tune of "This Old Man")

Feel the chill
In the air.
It is getting cold out there.
With a windy whoosh, the leaves are on the ground.
Soon we'll see snow coming down.

Readying for Winter
(sung to the tune of "The Farmer in the Dell")

The [squirrel hides some food].
The [squirrel hides some food].
Winter is on the way.
The [squirrel hides some food].

Sing additional verses, replacing the underlined phrase with phrases such as *chipmunk stores his seeds, beaver stores tree limbs,* and *bear eats lots of food.*

Try this:
- Color and cut out a copy of the winter animal cards on page 49. Use the cards to lead youngsters in singing each verse in the song.

- Write each child's name on a separate construction paper nut cutout. Store the nuts in a bag. For a quick time filler, remove a nut from the bag, announce the student's name, and have him pretend that he is a squirrel storing the nut for the winter while you lead youngsters in singing the song.

Wintertime

(sung to the tune of "Twinkle, Twinkle, Little Star")

Wintertime brings lots of snow.   *Flutter fingers.*
Winter's when the cold wind blows.   *Puff cheeks out.*
We make snowmen fat and round   *Build snowman.*
From the soft snow on the ground.   *Build snowman.*
Wintertime brings lots of snow.   *Flutter fingers.*
Winter's when the cold wind blows.   *Puff cheeks out.*

Try this:
● Have students hold the edges of a
bedsheet parachute-style, keeping the
sheet stretched tightly. Then drop foam
packing peanuts onto the sheet. Direct
youngsters to wiggle the sheet as they
sing the song.

Fun in the Snow

(sung to the tune of "The Farmer in the Dell")

We're [sledding down the hill].
We're [sledding down the hill].
Hi-ho, away we go.
We're [sledding down the hill].

Sing additional verses, replacing the underlined
phrase with phrases such as *skating on the
ice, skiing down the slope, making a snow fort,
building a snow pal,* and *rolling in the snow.*

Try this:
● Color and cut out a copy of the winter cards on
page 50. Use the cards to lead youngsters in
singing each verse in the song.

● Have the children act out the song as they sing.
For example, during the first verse have them
sit on the floor and lean to the left and right,
pretending to sled down a hill.

Up to the Hilltop

(sung to the tune of "Up on the Housetop")

Up to the hilltop, children climb
While they pull their sleds behind.
Over the snowdrifts, they slip and slide
Down to the bottom.
Oh! What a ride!

Snow, snow, snow,
Look at it blow.
Snow, snow, snow,
Who wouldn't go?

Up to the hilltop
Quick, quick, quick!
Down to the bottom
Lickety-split!

Try this:
● Invite two or three youngsters at a time to sit on a sled (or a large sled cutout) and pretend that they are riding on it while the class sings the song.

● Place masking tape across the floor to represent a hill. Encourage little ones to walk up and down the hill while singing the song.

Will the Snow Come Down?

(sung to the tune of "Do Your Ears Hang Low?")

Will the snow come down
From the sky and to the ground?
Will it fall and fall and fall
And then pile up very tall?
Can you build a snowy fort?
Make it tall or make it short.
Will the snow come down?

Try this:
● Encourage youngsters to drift like falling snowflakes while singing the song.

● Give each child a handful of fiberfill. As students sing, have them mold the fiberfill to resemble a snowball.

Dressing for Cold Weather
(sung to the tune of "The Hokey-Pokey")

You put your [snow boots] on.
You put your [snow boots] on.
You put your [snow boots] on,
And you [pull them up so tight].
Snowflakes keep on falling.
It is getting cold outside.
Time for some winter fun!

Sing additional verses, replacing the underlined text with the following:
jacket, button it up tight
snow hat, pull it down so tight
mittens, dance with such delight

Try this:
- Color and cut out a copy of the winter clothing cards on page 51. Before singing each verse, show students the corresponding card. As students sing, have them pretend to put on that article of clothing.

- Have each student sequence a cutout copy of the cards on page 51 in the order they would get dressed for cold weather. Then have students point to each card as they sing each verse.

Ten Cold Snowmen
(sung to the tune of "Ten Little Indians")

One cold, two cold, three cold snowmen,
Four cold, five cold, six cold snowmen,
Seven cold, eight cold, nine cold snowmen,
Ten cold snowmen in the snow.

One hot, two hot, three hot snowmen,
Four hot, five hot, six hot snowmen,
Seven hot, eight hot, nine hot snowmen,
Ten hot snowmen in the sun.

One wet, two wet, three wet snowmen,
Four wet, five wet, six wet snowmen,
Seven wet, eight wet, nine wet snowmen,
Ten wet snowmen on the ground.

Try this:
- Give each youngster a copy of the snowmen cards on page 52. Have him point to the corresponding snowmen while singing the song.

- Make ten snowmen and a sun cutout for your flannelboard. Place each snowman on the board during the first verse. During the second verse, place the sun on the board and point to each snowman in turn. During the last verse, remove one snowman at a time, changing the last line to "Ten wet snowmen melt away!"

Hanukkah Festivities

(sung to the tune of "The Wheels on the Bus")

On Hanukkah we light the candles,
Light the candles, light the candles.
On Hanukkah we light the candles
In our menorah.

On Hanukkah we eat some latkes,
Eat some latkes, eat some latkes.
On Hanukkah we eat some latkes
With some applesauce.

On Hanukkah we spin the dreidel,
Spin the dreidel, spin the dreidel.
On Hanukkah we spin the dreidel
With family and friends.

Christmastime

(sung to the tune of "Sing a Song of Sixpence")

Christmastime is coming.
It is almost here.
It's a holiday
That's filled with fun and cheer.
There are lots of presents
And lights upon the tree.
Christmastime is magical.
It's fun for you and me.

It's Santa!

(sung to the tune of "Bingo")

Who is that [jolly man in red]?
Ooh, aah! His name is Santa!
S-A-N-T-A
S-A-N-T-A
S-A-N-T-A
Oh yes, his name is Santa.

Sing additional verses, replacing the underlined phrase with phrases such as *with a big white beard, riding in a sleigh, checking off his list,* and *with a sack of toys.*

Try this:

● Give each student a copy of a Santa card from page 53. Have her point to the corresponding letters as she sings the song.

● Make a pretend version of Santa's sleigh by lining up eight chairs, two by two, for the reindeer. Place a ninth chair in the front for Rudolph and a tenth chair in the back for Santa. Then invite ten students at a time to pretend to be the reindeer and Santa during a singing of the song!

● Encourage youngsters to keep healthy and fit the way Santa needs to (to fit down those chimneys) by doing some "Santa-cizes"!

I'm a Reindeer

(sung to the tune of "I'm a Little Teapot")

I am Santa's reindeer,
Fast and strong!
I have two antlers and legs so long.
When I fly and pull ol' Santa's sleigh,
I'll bring you toys for Christmas day!

Try this:

● Help each youngster twist a brown pipe cleaner around one of his pointer fingers to resemble antlers. As you lead students in the song, have each child move his prop as desired.

On Christmas Day!

(sung to the tune of "The Wheels on the Bus")

The [lights] on the tree [go blink, blink, blink],
[Blink, blink, blink, blink, blink, blink].
The [lights] on the tree [go blink, blink, blink]
On Christmas day!

For verses 2–5, replace the underlined text
with the following:
    garland, is very long
    ornaments, are smooth and round
    tinsel, sways back and forth
    star, sits up on top

Verse 6:
The presents under the tree are all wrapped up,
All wrapped up, all wrapped up.
The presents under the tree are all wrapped up
On Christmas day!

Try this:
- Color and cut out a copy of the tree sequence cards on page 54. Use the cards to lead youngsters in singing each verse of the song.

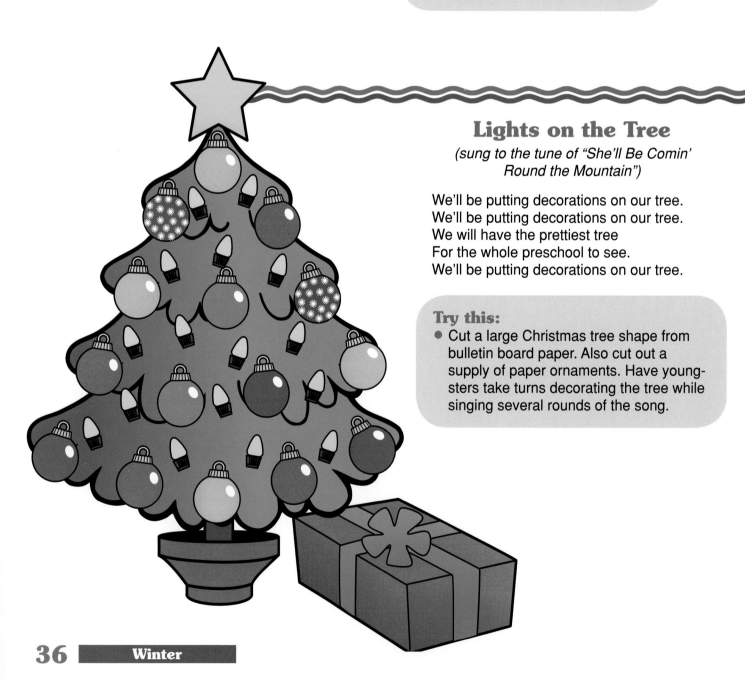

Lights on the Tree

(sung to the tune of "She'll Be Comin' Round the Mountain")

We'll be putting decorations on our tree.
We'll be putting decorations on our tree.
We will have the prettiest tree
For the whole preschool to see.
We'll be putting decorations on our tree.

Try this:
- Cut a large Christmas tree shape from bulletin board paper. Also cut out a supply of paper ornaments. Have youngsters take turns decorating the tree while singing several rounds of the song.

Holiday Cookies

(sung to the tune of "If You're Happy and You Know It")

If you're going to make some cookies, use your hands.
If you're going to make some cookies, use your hands.
Roll the dough out smooth and flat.
With your hands give it a pat.
If you're going to make some cookies, use your hands.

Try this:
- Give each youngster a ball of play dough. Have youngsters demonstrate each of the steps described in the song while they sing and pretend to make cookies.

Kwanzaa Time Is Here

(sung to the tune of "The Farmer in the Dell")

Kwanzaa time is here.
Kwanzaa time is here.
[Let's light the kinara!]
Kwanzaa time is here!

Sing additional verses, replacing the under-lined sentence with the following:
Lay down the mkeka.
Make a gift with your own hands.
Drink from the unity cup.

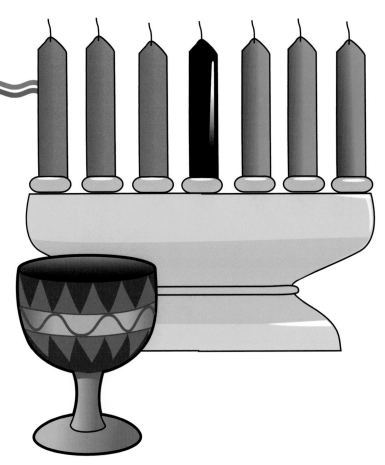

Happy New Year!

(sung to the tune of "The Itsy-Bitsy Spider")

New Year's Day has come and
We are glad it's here.
It is the beginning
Of a brand-new year.
We are happy on
This very special day.
Let's all celebrate—
The new year starts today!

Try this:
● Invite youngsters to wear New Year's party hats as they sing.

Martin Luther King Jr.'s Dreams

(sung to the tune of "Row, Row, Row Your Boat")

Peace, peace, peace and love,
Sweet equality.
These were Martin Luther King's
Dreams for you and me!

Try this:
● Have youngsters form a circle and hold hands as they sing the song.

Penguins at Play

Penguins live where it is cold
And swim in the big sea.
Penguins love to dive and fish.
They're cute as they can be.

Penguins waddle back and forth.
They're dressed in black and white.
They look like little men in suits.
They're such a funny sight.

Try this:
● Have youngsters waddle like penguins while reading the poem.

● Assemble between construction paper covers student copies of the booklet on pages 55 and 56. Have each student complete her booklet by writing her name on the cover and coloring the illustrations. Then help her use her booklet to follow along and read the first verse of the poem.

What a Penguin Does

(sung to the tune of "My Bonnie Lies Over the Ocean")

Oh, penguins swim in the ocean.
Oh, penguins slide on the ice.
Oh, penguins waddle when they walk.
Their black-and-white suits look so nice!

Penguins, penguins,
Oh, penguins live in the cold, the cold.
Penguins, penguins,
Oh, penguins live in the cold!

Polar Bears

(sung to the tune of "When the Saints Go Marching In")

The polar bears are big and white.
They live where there is cold and snow.
The polar bears are thick and furry
To keep warm when the cold winds blow.

North Pole

Polar Bear Poem

Polar bears live at the North Pole.
They swim and they fish all day.
Polar bears walk on the ice.
Their paws keep them from slipping away!

Wake Up, Groundhog!

(sung to the tune of the refrain from "Jingle Bells")

Ring! Ring! Ring!
Ring! Ring! Ring!
Groundhog, it's your day!
Time to wake and go outside.
Is winter going to stay? Hey!

Ring! Ring! Ring!
Ring! Ring! Ring!
Groundhog, it's your day!
If you see your dark shadow
Then springtime's far away!

I'm a Valentine

(sung to the tune of "I'm a Little Teapot")

I'm a valentine all trimmed in blue.
Here is my message written for you.
When you open me up, hear me say,
"I love you so on Valentine's Day!"

A Finger Heart

Fingers to fingers,

Thumb to thumb,

Bend them down,

And see what they become.

Dear Valentine,

I ♥ YOU!

Won't You Be Mine?

(sung to the tune of "I'm a Little Teapot")

Here's a special letter
Just for you.
I used some paper,
Glitter, and glue.
I hope that you will be mine on this day.
Friends forever,
Come let's play.

Try this:

● Write the song lyrics inside a heart
shape. Then copy a class supply on
red construction paper. Have each
child sign her name, decorate the
valentine with glitter, and present it—
in song—to her valentine.

Oh Valentine

(sung to the tune of "O Christmas Tree")

Oh valentine, oh valentine,
You are so special to me.
Oh valentine, oh valentine,
You are so special to me.
I made a card that's just for you.
It's made with hearts and flowers too.
Oh valentine, oh valentine,
You are so special to me.

Try this:

● Sing the song several times with students. Then have each youngster
decorate a paper heart shape to create a card. Encourage her to sing the
song and present the card to someone special on Valentine's Day.

● Make a class card adorned with hearts and flowers for a special member
of your school. Then change the *me* to *us* in the second, fourth, and last
lines, and the *I* to *we* in the fifth line of the song and have students sing to
that special someone when presenting her with the card.

Making a Card

Cut the paper.

Spread the glue.

Sprinkle the glitter.

I made it for you.

I'm a Little Cupid

(sung to the tune of "I'm a Little Teapot")

I'm a little cupid.
Don't you know?
I shoot love arrows; here is my bow.
With my little wings I fly above.
I make people fall in love!

Point to self.
Point outward.
Pretend to draw back bow.
Flap arms like wings.
Point to self; then place
  both hands over heart.

My Valentine Friend

(sung to the tune of the refrain from "Jingle Bells")

Valentine, valentine,
Please won't you be mine?
Lots of hugs and warm wishes
For you, my valentine!

Try this:
- Have each child color a personalized heart shape. Seat youngsters in a circle; then direct them to pass one of the hearts around the circle as they sing. When the song is over, ask the child holding the heart to say something sweet about the child whose name is on the heart. Then select a different heart to pass around the circle for another round of singing.

Valentine Fingerplay

If you'll be my valentine,
I'll give my heart to you.
I'll give you lots of great big hugs
And some sweet kisses too.
I'll send you hearts and candy
And valentine cards too.
Because you are my special friend,
Please know that I like you.

Arms out in front.
Hug yourself.
Purse lips.
Sweep arms in front.
Draw hearts in the air with fingers.
Hands over heart.
Extend hands outward.

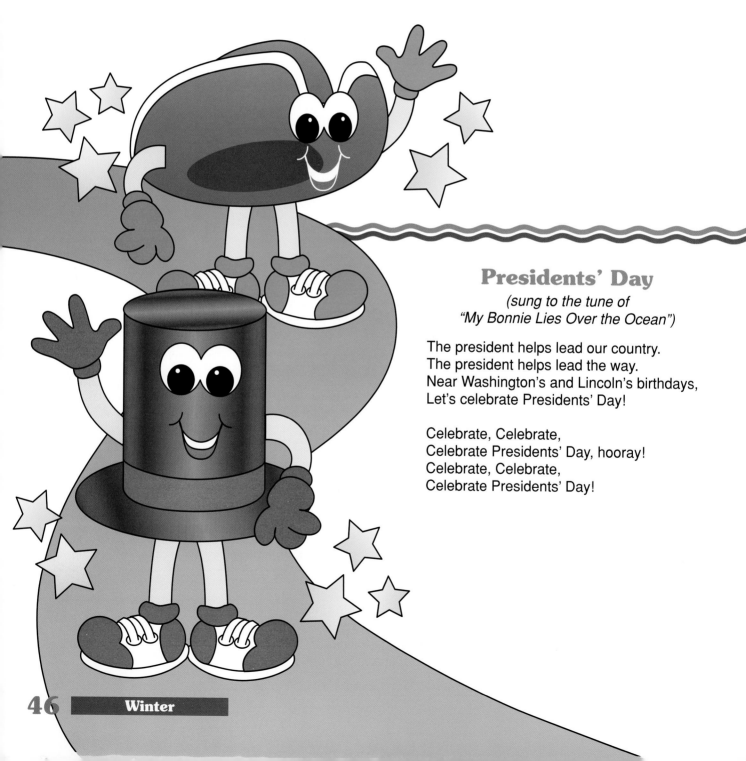

Presidents' Day

*(sung to the tune of
"My Bonnie Lies Over the Ocean")*

The president helps lead our country.
The president helps lead the way.
Near Washington's and Lincoln's birthdays,
Let's celebrate Presidents' Day!

Celebrate, Celebrate,
Celebrate Presidents' Day, hooray!
Celebrate, Celebrate,
Celebrate Presidents' Day!

Healthy Teeth

(sung to the tune of "The Hokey-Pokey")

You brush them up and down.
You brush them back and forth.
You brush them up and down,
And you brush them all around.
Then go and see your dentist.
He will check your teeth for you
And keep gums healthy too!

Try this:

- Cut out large white construction paper shapes to resemble supersize teeth. During several rounds of the song, invite youngsters, in turn, to use a small broom to demonstrate the motions of a toothbrush!

Do You Brush Your Teeth?

(sung to the tune of "Do Your Ears Hang Low?")

Do you brush your teeth?
Do you scrub until they shine?
Do you floss them every day?
Do you make them feel so fine?
Do you go and get a checkup,
Let your dentist check them out?
Do you brush your teeth?

Try this:

- After singing the song several times, give each student a copy of the daily brushing chart on page 57 to take home. Encourage youngsters to sing the song and demonstrate good brushing habits to an adult each day. Then have him draw a smiley face in the corresponding box to show that he brushed his teeth.

- Have students use hand motions while they sing the song to demonstrate that they know how to brush their teeth. Then reward each youngster with a copy of the badge on page 57.

It's a Winter Parade!

Plan a winter-themed parade with your youngsters! Have students make the props and accessories below. Then teach them the provided song and let the marching begin!

Props and Accessories

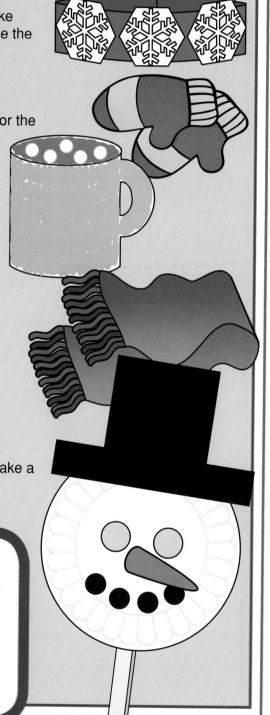

Snowflake Headband: Have each youngster glue snowflake cutouts to a construction paper strip. When the glue is dry, size the strip to fit the child's head.

Toasty Hands: Have each youngster wear colorful mittens for the parade!

Marvelous Marshmallows: Prepare a mug cutout for each child to color so that it appears as if it contains hot cocoa. Then encourage her to make white marshmallow prints in the hot cocoa.

Splendid Scarves: Have students don cozy scarves for the parade.

Snowpal Mask: Cut eyeholes in a paper plate for each child. Encourage him to glue facial features to the resulting mask to create a snowpal. Have him glue a hat cutout to the top of the mask. Then help him glue a jumbo craft stick to the mask to make a handle.

The Winter Parade Song
(sung to the tune of "When Johnny Comes Marching Home")

When all of the leaves fall from the trees we know, we know
That winter is here and soon we may have lots of snow!
We bundle up and we sled down hills,
And then so we do not get the chills,
We will drink hot cocoa. Winter is here—hurray!

Winter Cards

Use with "Fun in the Snow" on page 31.

TEC61075

TEC61075

TEC61075

TEC61075

TEC61075

TEC61075

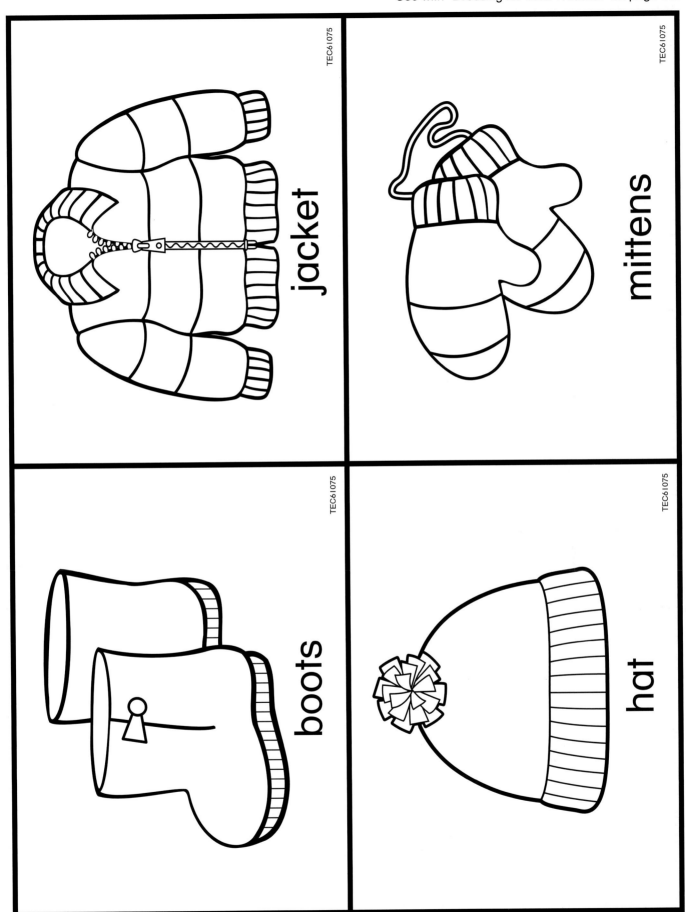

jacket

mittens

boots

hat

Snowmen Cards

Use with "Ten Cold Snowmen" on page 33.

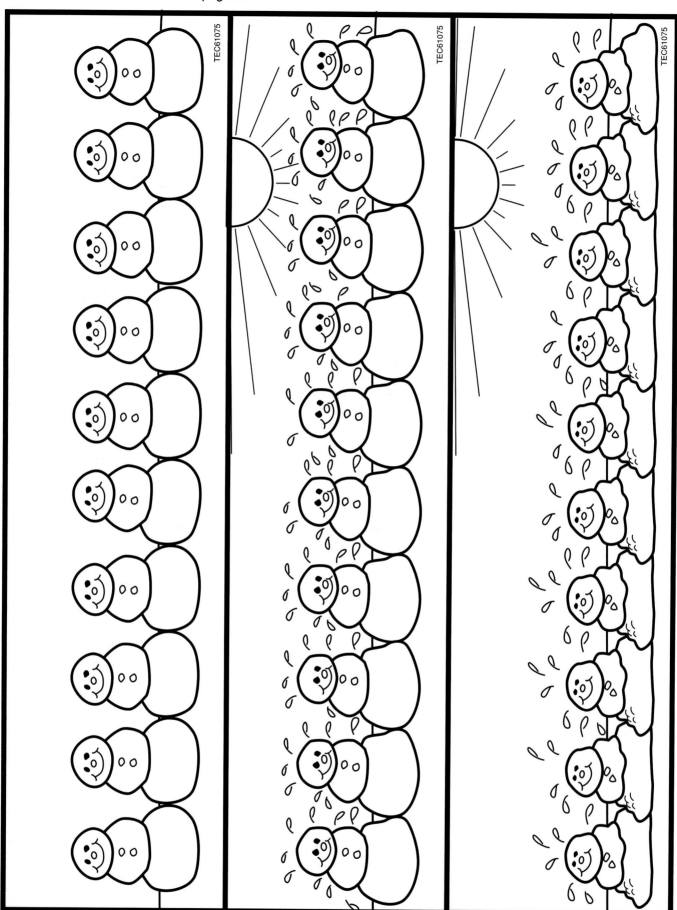

TEC61075

TEC61075

TEC61075

Tree Sequence Cards
Use with "On Christmas Day!" on page 36.

TEC61075

TEC61075

TEC61075

TEC61075

TEC61075

TEC61075

Penguins live where it is cold

©The Mailbox® • *Songs & Rhymes on Parade* • TEC61075

1

And swim in the big sea.

2

Penguins love to dive and fish.

3

They're cute as they can be.

4

Keep Those Teeth Healthy!

Monday	Tuesday	Wednesday	Thursday	Friday	Saturday	Sunday

©The Mailbox® • Songs & Rhymes on Parade • TEC61075

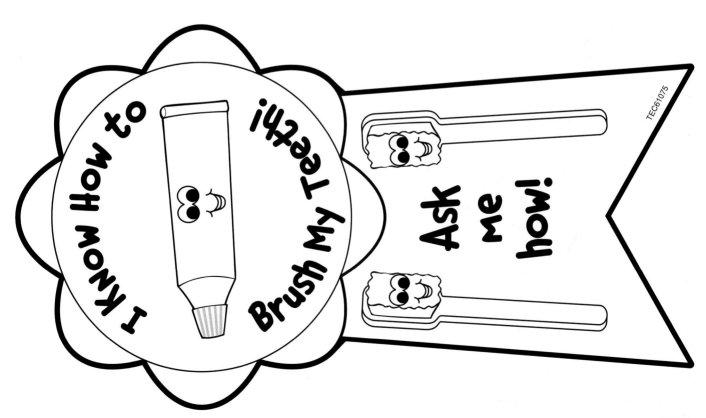

I Know How to Brush My Teeth!

Ask me how!

TEC61075

Spring

Green Eggs and Ham
(sung to the tune of "Three Blind Mice")

Green eggs and ham,
Green eggs and ham,
From Sam-I-am,
From Sam-I-am.
I will eat them in a [boat].
I will eat them with a [goat].
I will eat them here and there.
Green eggs and ham.

Try this:
- To celebrate Dr. Seuss's birthday (March 2), share one of his most popular books—*Green Eggs and Ham.* Then lead students in singing the above song.

- Color and cut out a copy of the rhyming picture cards on page 79. Sing the song and hold up the boat and goat cards. Repeat the song, substituting a different rhyming pair each time.

March Weather
(sung to the tune of "My Bonnie Lies Over the Ocean")

In March there is all kinds of weather,
From snow to rain and warm sunshine.
It ends as a nice gentle lamb,
But comes roaring in like a lion.

Try this:
- For each child, attach a lion cutout to one side of a craft stick handle and a lamb cutout to the other side. Have each youngster display the correct side of her resulting puppet during the last two lines of the song.

- Each morning during March, lead little ones in singing the song. Then record the day's weather. Is it a lion or lamb day? At the end of the month, help youngsters determine whether there were more lion or lamb days.

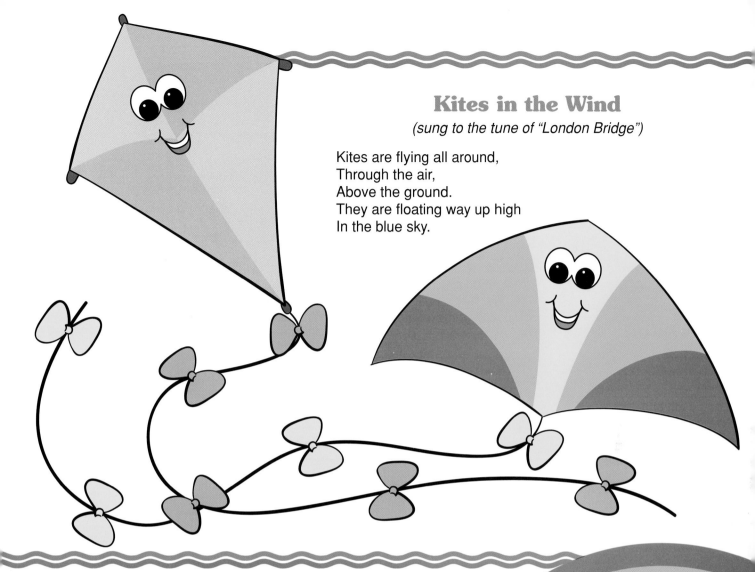

Kites in the Wind
(sung to the tune of "London Bridge")

Kites are flying all around,
Through the air,
Above the ground.
They are floating way up high
In the blue sky.

St. Patrick's Day
(sung to the tune of "When the Saints Go Marching In")

St. Patrick's Day is here again.
We wear our shamrocks and our green.
We look for pots of gold and rainbows.
They are the brightest we have seen!

Try this:
- Invite a child to be the leprechaun. Have the leprechaun close her eyes while you choose a child to hide a pot-of-gold cutout behind his back. Everyone sings the song while the leprechaun looks for the gold.

Tiny Leprechaun

(sung to the tune of "This Old Man")

Leprechaun,
Dressed in green,
Tiniest man you've ever seen!
With a pot of gold at the end of the rainbow,
He'll never let you catch him, no!

Try this:

● Make a simple leprechaun stick puppet and a pot-of-gold stick puppet using the patterns on page 80. As the class sings the song, bring each puppet out one at a time from behind your back, and then hide them again during the last line of the song as you would for "Where Is Thumbkin?"

● At the conclusion of the song, have little ones suggest ways to catch a leprechaun.

● While singing the song, invite students to tiptoe like leprechauns secretly moving their pots of gold.

It Is Springtime Now

(sung to the tune of "Do Your Ears Hang Low?")

It is springtime now,
And the grass is green and new.
Pretty flowers bloom,
And the springtime rains fall too.
Buzzing bees fly round
Over flowers in the ground.
It is springtime now.

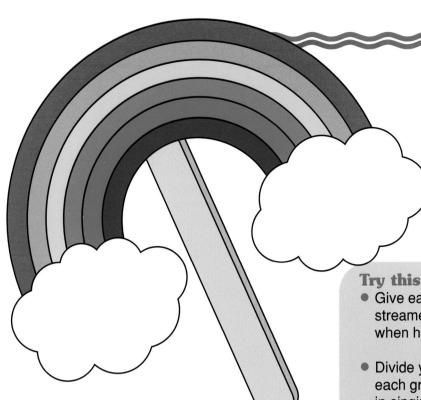

Colors in the Rainbow
(sung to the tune of "Ten Little Indians")

Red and orange and then there's yellow,
Green and blue and then there's violet.
These are all the pretty colors
We see in a rainbow!

Try this:
- Give each child a length of a rainbow-colored streamer. Have each youngster wave his strip when he hears his color in the song.

- Divide youngsters into six groups and assign each group a color from the song. Lead the class in singing the song twice, the first time having each group stand when its color is sung and the second time having the group sit back down.

- Give each child a rainbow stick puppet to use as a song prop. As you lead little ones in singing the song, encourage them to point to each color on their puppets.

The Rain in the Spring
(sung to the tune of "The Wheels on the Bus")

The rain in the spring goes drip, drip, drop,
Drip, drip, drop, drip, drip, drop.
The rain in the spring goes drip, drip, drop
All day long!

Suggestions for additional verses:
The flowers in the spring all grow, grow, grow.
The wind in the spring goes swish, swish, swish.

Muddy Days

(sung to the tune of "The Itsy-Bitsy Spider")

Mud is wet and messy
But fun to play in too.
I squish it through my fingers
And make a pie for you.
When it gets all sunny,
The mud will go away.
And then we'll have to wait until
It rains again someday.

Try this:
- Prior to singing the song, partially fill a gallon-size resealable plastic bag with dirt. Ask youngsters what they think will happen when you add water. Add some water and securely seal the bag. Then lead students in singing the song as they pass the bag around and squish the bag to make mud.

- Invite little ones to use play dough to make pretend mud pies as they sing the song.

Ten Little Bunnies

(sung to the tune of "Ten Little Indians")

One little, two little, three little bunnies,   *Add fingers one at a time as you sing.*
Four little, five little, six little bunnies,
Seven little, eight little, nine little bunnies,
Ten little bunnies in a row.   *Wiggle all ten fingers.*

Ten little, nine little, eight little bunnies,   *Take away one finger at a time.*
Seven little, six little, five little bunnies,
Four little, three little, two little bunnies,
One little bunny by herself. Oh, no!   *Wiggle one finger.*

One little, two little… (Count quickly to ten.)   *Add fingers again.*
Ten little bunnies in a row!   *Wiggle all ten fingers.*

Fluffy Rabbit

I have a little rabbit
Whose tail is fluffy white.
Hippity-hop, hippity-hop
He goes all day and night.

Baby Bunny

Baby bunny, hop around.
Baby bunny, touch the ground.

Baby bunny, stand up tall.
Baby bunny, get oh so small.

Baby bunny, touch your toes.
Baby bunny, wiggle your nose.

Baby bunny, jump up high.
Baby bunny, wave bye-bye.

Try this:

● Make a simple bunny ear headband for each child. Have youngsters wear their bunny ears and pretend to be rabbits as they act out the motion for each line of the rhyme.

● After little ones are familiar with the rhyme, recite it again, inviting them to complete the second line (rhyme) in each stanza.

● Pair students to create bunny buddies. As the class recites the poem together, have one student perform the first motion and the other perform the second motion in each stanza.

Hippity-Hop

I'm a little brown bunny
With a fluffy, white tail.

I hippity-hop, hippity-hop
Over hill and dale.

I hope to meet a bunny friend
Who'll want to run and play

So we can hippity-hop around
This sunny springtime day.

Try this:
- Have each child glue a cotton ball tail to a bunny cutout. Then encourage students to use their bunnies to act out the poem.

- Use masking tape to mark off a trail through your classroom or in the school gym. Have each of your little ones pretend to be a bunny and hop along the trail as the class recites the rhyme.

Eggs in My Basket

(sung to the tune of "Skip to My Lou")

Eggs, eggs, Easter eggs,
Eggs, eggs, Easter eggs,
Eggs, eggs, Easter eggs,
So pretty in my basket!

I see [pink, blue, and green].
I see [pink, blue, and green].
I see [pink, blue, and green].
Pretty eggs in my basket!

Repeat the second verse, substituting other color words for the underlined words.

Try this:
- Hide plastic eggs around the room and have little ones collect the eggs in baskets as they sing the song.

- Have students pretend to pick up eggs and put them in imaginary baskets as they sing the song.

Easter Eggs

(sung to the tune of the refrain from "Jingle Bells")

Easter eggs, Easter eggs,
Pink and orange and green—
These are just the nicest eggs
That I have ever seen.

Easter eggs, Easter eggs,
Purple, yellow, blue—
I have lots of Easter eggs,
So I'll share some with you!

Try this:
- Give each child an egg cutout in a color featured in the song. Then have each child hold up her egg cutout when she hears her egg's color in the song.

It's Hatching!

(sung to the tune of "Up on the Housetop")

Tucked in a nest, a small egg lays
Warm and snug for days and days.
Then one bright morning, a crack is heard!
Out pops a tiny, yellow bird!

Peep! Peep! Peep! He wants to go!
Peep! Peep! Peep! He wants to go!
Out of the nest the chick hops, then
Runs quick to safety with mother hen.

Try this:

- Encourage little ones to pretend to be the chick hatching out of the egg as they sing the song.

- Share with children a book about chicks hatching, such as *From Egg to Chicken* by Robin Nelson, *Hatching Chicks* by Susan Blackaby, or *Where Do Chicks Come From?* by Amy E. Sklansky.

Catching Butterflies

(sung to the tune of "A-hunting We Will Go")

A-hunting we will go.
A-hunting we will go.
We'll catch a little butterfly,
And then we'll let it go.

Try this:

- Choose two children to stand facing one another, hold hands, and raise their arms as if for "London Bridge." Have the rest of the class form a line of butterflies and march in a circle underneath the "net" as they sing. On the word *catch,* the net's arms come down carefully around one of the butterflies until they release it on the words *let it go.*

- Have students stand in a circle and pass around a butterfly cutout as they sing the song. The child holding the butterfly when *go* is sung in the last line sits down. Continue singing and having students pass the butterfly until everyone is seated.

From Egg to Butterfly

I'm an egg as quiet as can be.

I'm a caterpillar crawling up a tree.

I'm a chrysalis. What's inside of me?

I'm a butterfly flying so free.

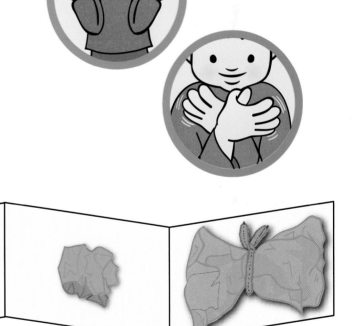

Try this:
- Give each child a paper strip that has been accordion-folded into fourths. Have him glue a small tissue paper ball into the first section for the egg. In the second section, have him glue a small piece of pipe cleaner for the caterpillar. For the chrysalis, direct him to glue a larger tissue paper ball to the third section. In the final section, help him use a rectangular piece of colorful tissue paper and a piece of pipe cleaner to fashion a butterfly. Then have students point to the corresponding stages on their projects as you lead them in reciting the rhyme.

Friendly Butterfly

A black and orange butterfly
Flitted all around.

She flitted round the garden,
Then landed on the ground.

She stayed there for a moment,
Then took off again

And fluttered to the flowers
To join her many friends.

Flutter fingers to a neighbor.

Try this:
- Invite half the class to flutter around the classroom like butterflies as the remainder of the class recites the rhyme. Then have youngsters switch roles.

The Pond
(sung to the tune of "He's Got the Whole World in His Hands")

Out in the pond, you'll find some [fish].
Out in the pond, you'll find some [fish].
Out in the pond, you'll find some [fish].
Out in the pond, you'll find some [fish].

Repeat the song, substituting other pond animals—such as frogs, snails, turtles, and ducks—for the underlined word.

Try this:
- Color and cut out a copy of the pond animal cards on page 81. Sing the song and hold up the fish card as you sing. Repeat the song, holding up another animal card each time you sing.

- Place a large pond cutout on the floor. Give each child a pond animal card from page 81. As you lead youngsters in singing the song, have each child place his critter in the pond when he hears its name.

Tadpoles to Frogs
(sung to the tune of "Twinkle, Twinkle, Little Star")

Little tadpoles hatch from eggs.
They get bigger and grow legs.
Then their tails will shorten too,
Making frogs that are brand-new.
Frogs use legs to swim around
And to jump upon the ground.

Try this:
- Give each child a cutout copy of the frog life cycle cards on page 80. Help students put their own cards in order as they sing the song.

- During the first three lines of the song, have youngsters lie on their tummies and wiggle like tadpoles. Then invite them to hop around like frogs during the remainder of the song.

I'm a Duck

I fly with my wings.
I paddle with my feet.
I quack with my beak.
I'm a duck—how neat!

Tuck hands in underarms and flap.
Paddle hands.
Make a beak with hand.
Point to self and give a thumbs-up.

Try this:
- Chant the rhyme this time with an enthusiastic, marching beat. Have the students repeat each line after you in a call-and-response format.

Little Turtle
(sung to the tune of "I'm a Little Teapot")

I'm a little turtle in a pond.
Of the water, I am fond.
This is where I live and eat and play
With my turtle friends all day.

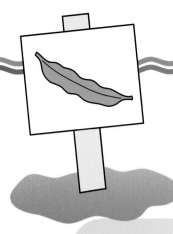
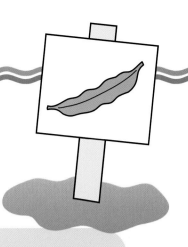

Dirt, Dirt, Dirt

I plant a seed in the dirt, dirt, dirt.
I pull a weed from the dirt, dirt, dirt.
I see some green in the dirt, dirt, dirt.
I grew some beans in the dirt, dirt, dirt.

Try this:
- Have little ones act out each line of the rhyme by patting the floor three times as they say, "Dirt, dirt, dirt."

- Divide the class into four groups and assign each group a different line from the rhyme and a corresponding motion. Have youngsters perform their motions when it's their turn.

Our Garden

(sung to the tune of "Row, Row, Row Your Boat")

Dig, dig, dig the soil.
Drop a seed right in.
Cover it; water it; give it sun.
Our garden begins!

Try this:
- Have students sing the song as they plant seeds in paper cups filled with soil.

- After singing the song, ask little ones to imagine that they have a garden of their own. Engage them in a discussion of what they would like to grow in their imaginary gardens.

Little Seed

I'm a little round seed buried underground,
As small as a tiny ball.

I sit here and wait for the sun and the rain
To make me grow big and tall.

The rain pours down; the sun shines bright.
My roots begin to grow.

My stem and leaves reach for the sky.
I'm a sunflower, don't you know?

Try this:
- Make simple cutouts of a seed, roots, a stem, leaves, and a sunflower bloom. As you recite the rhyme with the class, display each cutout during the corresponding line.

I Love My Garden

(sung to the tune of "A Tisket, a Tasket")

My garden, my garden,
I love my veggie garden!
With [squash and beans and cucumbers],
I love my veggie garden!

My garden, my garden,
I love my flower garden!
With [tulips, roses, and some mums],
I love my flower garden!

Repeat either verse as desired, substituting other plant names for the underlined words.

From Seed to Flower

(sung to the tune of "The Farmer in the Dell")

The gardener plants the seeds.
The gardener plants the seeds.
Hi-ho, the derry-o!
The gardener plants the seeds.

Continue with these verses:
The sun shines warm and bright.
The rain falls gently down.
The seeds begin to sprout.
The flowers start to bloom.

Try this:

● Sing the song and have the class pretend to be seeds. During the corresponding song verses, act as the gardener, sun, and rain while youngsters sprout and grow.

● Seat youngsters in a circle. As the class sings the first verse, choose three children to sit in the center of the circle and be the seeds. Choose another child to be the gardener. During the second verse, have the gardener choose another child to be the sun. The sun comes in to shine on the seeds and the gardener goes out. The sun chooses the rain in the third verse, and then the seeds "sprout and grow" in the fourth and fifth verses.

Creepy Crawlers

(sung to the tune of "Pawpaw Patch")

Worm and spider,
Bee and beetle,
Slug and snail and
Caterpillar—
Where are all these
Creepy crawlers?
Right here in my garden!

Try this:

● Assemble student copies of the booklet on pages 82 and 83. Have each student complete his booklet by writing his name and coloring the illustrations. Then help him use the booklet to "read" the words to the song.

● After singing the song, provide children with various tactile materials, such as craft foam, pipe cleaners, packing peanuts, aluminum foil, and pom-poms. Encourage them to create their own creepy crawlers to use as props during additional singings.

Buggy Bugs

Bugs can be little
Like dots in the sand.
Some have wide wings
And are bigger than your hand.
Some bugs will shimmer
In the bright light.
While others just blink
In the very dark night.

Insect Song

(sung to the tune of "For He's a Jolly Good Fellow")

A [beetle] is an insect.
A [beetle] is an insect.
A [beetle] is an insect.
All insects have six legs!

Sing the song several more times, substituting "beetle" with the name of other insects, such as *housefly, butterfly, ant, mosquito,* or *firefly.*

Try this:
- On the board, draw a simple beetle without its legs. At the end of the song, invite student volunteers to come up and draw six legs on the beetle or have the class count to six as you add the legs to the drawing.

A Ladybug Poem

Along came a ladybug that landed on me.
She crawled on my finger and it tickled, you see!
Then, all of a sudden, she just flew away,
And I called to her, "Come back some other day!"

Try this:
- While reciting the poem, have each youngster act it out using a red pom-pom as a ladybug prop.

Buzz, Buzz, Buzz

(sung to the tune of the refrain from "Jingle Bells")

Buzz, buzz, buzz! Buzz, buzz, buzz!
You're busy little bees!
Bring some nectar to your hive.
Make honey if you please!

Try this:
● Place a honey-covered piece of bread at each child's table area. As you lead students in singing the song, have them move like bees to their tables and eat their snacks.

Five Little Flowers

Five little flowers growing happy as can be.
The first one said, "A drink of water's good for me!"
The second one said, "I've got petals and a stem."
The third one said, "I have leaves and I like them."
The fourth one said, "How I love the warm sun."
Then the fifth one said, "Growing big is so much fun!"

Try this:
● Have youngsters hold up the correct number of fingers to correspond to each line of the rhyme.

● Prepare five blossom cutouts and five stems for flannelboard use. Place the five stems on the board. Have student volunteers add a blossom for each corresponding line of the rhyme.

The Bird Song

(sung to the tune of "The Farmer in the Dell")

Birdies hatch from eggs.
They grow and learn to fly.
They eat worms and bugs and seeds
And fly across the sky!

Squat down and break out of egg.
Slowly stand and flap wings.
Bend at waist as if pecking food.
Flap wings and move around room.

Happy Mother's Day!

Mother dear, I love you, and I know you love me too.
I am very glad to celebrate this holiday with you!
I thank you for the things you do, and I just want to say,
"I hope you have a superspecial, happy Mother's Day!"

Try this:

● Invite mothers or other special females in your youngsters' lives in for refreshments. Have the class perform the poem and then give hugs to their special guests.

● Divide the class into three groups. Have each group recite one of the first three lines from the poem. Then invite all the groups to enthusiastically recite the last line together.

It's a Spring Parade!

Plan a spring-themed parade with your youngsters! Have students make the props and accessories below. Then teach them the provided song and let the marching begin!

Props and Accessories

Duckling Headbands: Have each youngster color duckling cutouts and then glue them in a row to a construction paper strip. Staple the strip to fit the child's head.

Baskets of Eggs: Invite little ones to place plastic eggs in baskets and then carry the baskets during the parade!

Muddy Puddles: Place a dollop of brown fingerpaint on a sheet of blue paper for each youngster. Invite students to fingerpaint until a desired effect is achieved. When the paint is dry, trim the papers so they resemble muddy puddles.

Bunny Headbands: Have each student glue a brown bunny cutout to a construction paper strip. Help him glue green crinkled paper shreds around the bunny. Then staple the strip to fit the youngster's head.

Raindrop Danglers: Have each youngster add glitter to raindrop cutouts. Then invite him to glue cotton batting to a gray cloud cutout. Next, help students tape a length of curling ribbon to each raindrop and then attach the remaining ends to the cloud cutout.

The Spring Parade Song
(sung to the tune of "When Johnny Comes Marching Home")

The ducklings are hatching from their eggs. It's spring! It's spring!
The calves walk around on wobbly legs. It's spring! It's spring!
The leaves all grow and the flowers bud.
The rain falls down and makes lots of mud.
There are chocolate bunnies. Spring is the best. Hooray!

TEC61075

TEC61075

TEC61075

TEC61075

TEC61075

TEC61075

Leprechaun and Pot-of-Gold Patterns
Use with "Tiny Leprechaun" on page 60.

Frog Life Cycle Cards
Use with "Tadpoles to Frogs" on page 69.

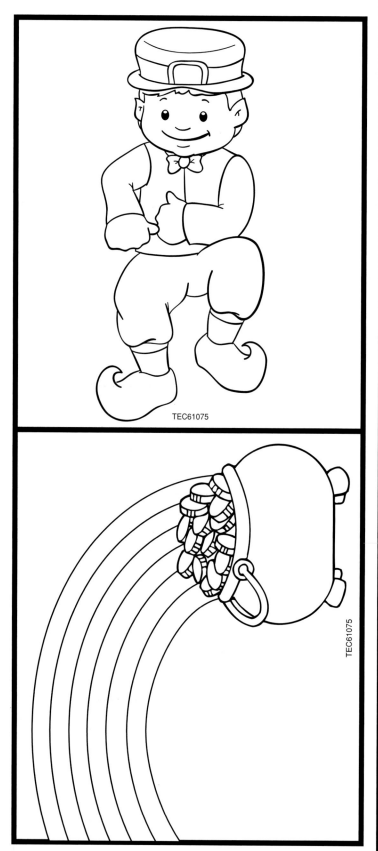

TEC61075

TEC61075

TEC61075

TEC61075

TEC61075

TEC61075

TEC61075

TEC61075

CREEPY CRAWLERS

Name _____

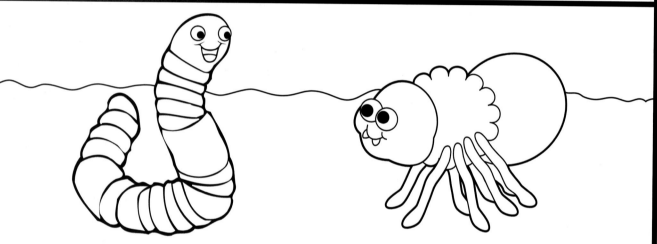

Worm and spider,

1

Bee and beetle,

2

Slug and snail and caterpillar—

3

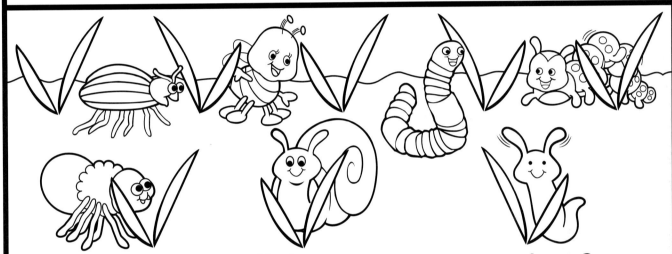

Where are all these creepy crawlers?

4

Right here in my garden!

5

Summer

Graduation Time

(sung to the tune of "Twinkle, Twinkle, Little Star")

Graduation time is here.
It's the end of our school year.
We learned new things every day,
In our work and in our play.
Graduation time is here.
It's the best day of the year!

Try this:

● Prior to singing the song, invite youngsters to name things they learned throughout the year, such as new letters, how to share, or how to play a game. Then lead students in singing the song, ending it with a big cheer.

I Love Daddy!

(sung to the tune of "For He's a Jolly Good Fellow")

I have the very best daddy!
I have the very best daddy!
I have the very best daddy!
And I love him so!

And I love him so!
And I love him so!

On Father's Day I will tell him.
On Father's Day I will tell him.
On Father's Day I will tell him
That I love him so!

Try this:

● To highlight another special male caregiver, a child simply substitutes the caregiver's title at the end of each of the first three lines.

● At the end of the song, invite youngsters to share why they think they have the very best daddies.

Summer Fun

(sung to the tune of "My Bonnie Lies Over the Ocean")

Summer is very exciting!
It's when we have fun, you will see.
We [swim] and we [camp] in the summer.
It is the best season to me!

Sing additional verses, replacing the underlined words with other summer activity words, such as *hike, read, fish, eat,* and *play.*

Sunny Day Play!

(sung to the tune of "This Old Man")

In the sun, in the sun,
We go out and have some fun!
On a sunny day there is lots and lots to do!
I like [swimming]. How 'bout you?

Try this:

● Invite students to share their favorite summer activities. Then substitute those activities as you lead the class in singing additional verses.

● Choose a word to substitute in the blank. Whisper it in a child's ear. Encourage him to act out the word at the appropriate part of the song. Challenge his classmates to guess the action and finish the song.

Summertime Rhyme

(sung to the tune of "Miss Mary Mack")

It's summertime, time, time,
So let's all rhyme, rhyme, rhyme!
Oh, can you find, find, find
What rhymes with [sand, sand, sand]?   *Youngsters name words that rhyme with sand.*

Insert a different summertime word in the blank each time you lead the class in singing the song.

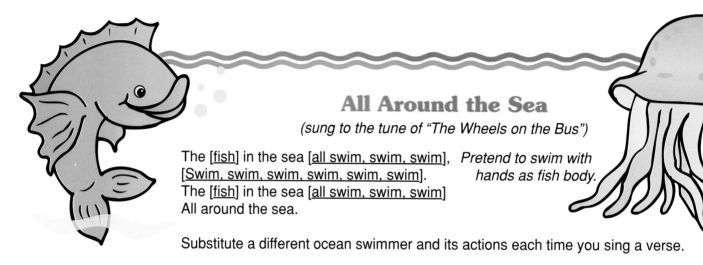

All Around the Sea

(sung to the tune of "The Wheels on the Bus")

The [fish] in the sea [all swim, swim, swim],   *Pretend to swim with*
[Swim, swim, swim, swim, swim, swim].   *hands as fish body.*
The [fish] in the sea [all swim, swim, swim]
All around the sea.

Substitute a different ocean swimmer and its actions each time you sing a verse.

The lobster…goes pinch, pinch, pinch.   *Pinch with fingers.*
The crab…goes crawl, crawl, crawl.   *Crawl up arm with fingers.*
The whale…goes blow, blow, blow.   *Blow water from top of head with*
          hands.

The dolphin…goes jump, jump, jump.   *Make diving motion with arms.*
The shark…goes chomp, chomp, chomp.   *Make biting motion with arms.*
The jellyfish… goes wiggle, wiggle, wiggle.   *Wiggle body.*
The diver… goes look, look, look.   *Hold imaginary diver's mask in front of*
          eyes.

Try this:
- Color and cut out a copy of the picture cards on pages 93–94. As you lead youngsters in singing each verse, hold up the corresponding card and encourage students to move like the featured animal or diver.

- Put a copy of the picture cards (pages 93–94) in a beach bag. Invite youngsters to take turns picking a card and leading the next verse.

Down in the Ocean

(sung to the tune of "Down by the Station")

Down in the ocean
Early in the morning.
See the little [lobster]
[Crawling] around.
See the little [lobster]
[Crawling] in the ocean.
[Crawl, crawl, pinch, pinch].
Off it goes!

Substitute a different ocean swimmer and its actions each time you sing a verse.

Octopus…waving…wave, wave, squirt, squirt
Dolphin…jumping… jump, jump, splash, splash
Diver…looking…look, look, swim, swim

Try this:
- When little ones are familiar with the song, encourage them to act out the motions of each ocean swimmer during the corresponding verse.

Ice Cream

I like my ice cream on a stick.
It's the only kind I pick.
But when the sun is really hot,
I have to lick it quite a lot!

Try this:
- At the end of the song, ask youngsters to describe what happens to ice cream on a hot day. Then place a frozen treat in a sunny location and another one in a shady or cooler location. Invite little ones to observe the two treats. Which one melts faster?

- Have students vote on their favorite way to eat ice cream: on a stick, on a cone, or in a bowl.

My Popsicle Treat

I have a Popsicle treat with two sticks—
One on the left and one on the right.

I know I want to eat it now,
But which side should I bite?

Try this:
- Make a construction paper Popsicle treat for each student with two craft sticks attached to each one. Label the sticks with the words *right* and *left.* Reinforce right and left with students while they hold their Popsicle treats and recite the poem.

- Ask little ones to decide which side of the Popsicle treat they would like to bite first. Then take a class vote.

Banana Split

(sung to the tune of "The Farmer in the Dell")

[Make a banana split.]
[Make a banana split.]
Time to eat a yummy treat!
[Make a banana split.]

Continue the song by substituting the underlined phrase with the following toppings. Encourage youngsters to add the corresponding motion for each verse.

Add a banana—slice!	*Pretend to slice a banana.*
Add the ice cream—scoop!	*Make a scooping motion with hand.*
Add the topping—pour!	*Pretend to pour on the topping.*
Add the whipped cream—squirt!	*Put hands together as if squirting.*
Add the sprinkles—shake!	*Pretend to shake sprinkles on.*
Take a big bite—yum!	*Pretend to use a spoon to take a bite.*

Try this:
- Color and cut out each banana split item from the patterns on page 95. Prepare each cutout for flannelboard use. As you sing the first verse, place the dish cutout near the bottom of the board. Then, during each remaining verse, add the corresponding ingredient, concluding with the spoon.

The Ice-Cream Truck Is Coming!

*(sung to the tune of
"She'll Be Comin' Round the Mountain")*

Oh, the ice-cream truck is comin' down the street!
Oh, the ice-cream truck is comin' down the street!
Oh, it makes my skin just tingle
When I hear that jingle, jingle!
Oh, the ice-cream truck is comin' down the street!

Picnic Packing

(sung to the tune of "For He's a Jolly Good Fellow")

We're going on a picnic!
We're going on a picnic!
We're going on a picnic!
And I'll bring something [red].

I will pack some [apples].
I will pack some [apples].
I will pack some [apples]
Because [apples] are [red].

Sing additional verses, replacing the color word and food each time.
Suggestions include: *blue, berries; yellow, bananas; brown, cookies;
green, celery; orange, carrots.*

Try this:

- Gather play foods and other picnic items—such as a napkin, cup,
  ball, plate, or flyswatter—that are (or are close to) a solid color.
  Place the items in a picnic basket. Sing the first verse with a
  desired color word. Have a volunteer choose an item of that color
  from the basket. The class sings the second verse and inserts the
  name of the chosen item.

- Give each youngster a paper plate and encourage him to draw a
  food in each of the following colors: red, yellow, and green. Sing the
  first verse with one of the three colors. Then select a youngster to
  share her picnic food of that color and have the class finish the song.
  Repeat the second verse with different volunteers. Then repeat
  the activity by substituting a different color word in the first verse.

The Best Summer Fruit
(sung to the tune of "Skip to My Lou")

[Eat, eat, watermelon.]
[Eat, eat, watermelon.]
[Eat, eat, watermelon],
The best summer fruit, yeah!

Continue with additional verses, replacing the underlined phrase with the phrases below

Green, green on the outside.
Red, red on the inside.
Spit, spit, spit the seeds out!

Watermelon Treat
(sung to the tune of "Twinkle, Twinkle, Little Star")

Watermelon on the vine,
Watermelon tastes so fine!
On the outside green and round,
Red inside where seeds are found.
Watermelon, cold and sweet,
Watermelon—what a treat!
Yum!

Try this:
- Assemble student copies of the booklet on pages 96–97. Have each student complete her booklet by writing her name and coloring the illustrations. Then help her use the booklet to "read" the song.

- Make simple cutouts of a watermelon vine, a whole watermelon, a watermelon half, and a slice with a big bite taken out. Prepare the cutouts for flannelboard use. Then stack them atop each other on the board, with the vine on the top of the stack and the bitten melon on the bottom. As you lead the class in singing, remove each cutout after the corresponding line to reveal the next one underneath.

Let's Hear It for the USA

(sung to the tune of "When Johnny Comes Marching Home")

Let's hear it for the USA! Hurrah! Hurrah!
Let's hear it for the USA! Hurrah! Hurrah!
We celebrate July the Fourth
With fireworks, picnics, and flags, of course!
'Cause we love our country—
Hurrah for red, white, and blue!

Try this:
- Tape one-foot lengths of red, white, and blue ribbon or crepe paper streamers to the end of a craft stick for each child. Invite students to wave their sticks and march while singing the song.

Fourth of July

(sung to the tune of "The Mulberry Bush")

Fourth of July is coming soon
With picnics, parades, and fireworks too.
Let's celebrate the day today
With red and white and blue!

Try this:
- Tape a class supply of red, white, and blue construction paper squares in a circle on the floor. As the song is sung, little ones march around the circle. At the end of the song, each child stops at the closest square and, in turn, identifies her color.

It's a Summer Parade!

Plan a summer-themed parade with your youngsters! Have students make the props and accessories below. Then teach them the provided song and let the marching begin!

Props and Accessories

Sand and Swim Props: Have students carry sand buckets and scoops. Encourage youngsters to wear sunglasses, beach hats, and shorts.

Ice-Cream Art: Tint a mixture of shaving cream and white glue. Have each youngster glue a construction paper cone cutout to a 12" x 18" sheet of paper. Then have her spoon the shaving cream mixture above the cone. When the mixture dries, it looks like fruity soft-serve ice cream!

Hot Dog Headband: Make a simple hot dog and bun cutout. Have a youngster squirt red and yellow paint over the hot dog to resemble ketchup and mustard. Then invite her to sprinkle green confetti relish over the toppings. When the project is dry, have her glue it to a construction paper strip; then staple the strip to fit her head.

Sun Masks: Cut eyeholes in a yellow disposable paper plate for each child. Then have each youngster glue orange triangle cutouts to his plate to resemble sun rays. Finally, instruct him to glue a jumbo craft stick to the plate to make a handle.

The Summer Parade Song
(sung to the tune of "When Johnny Comes Marching Home")

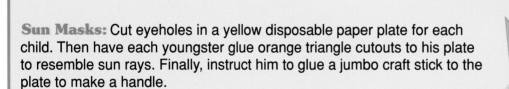

When summer is here, it's very hot. Oh yes—it's hot!
We picnic outside and eat things that we like—a lot!
We love to swim and play in the sand.
Oh yes, we think summertime is grand!
And we all eat ice cream. Summer's the best—hurray!

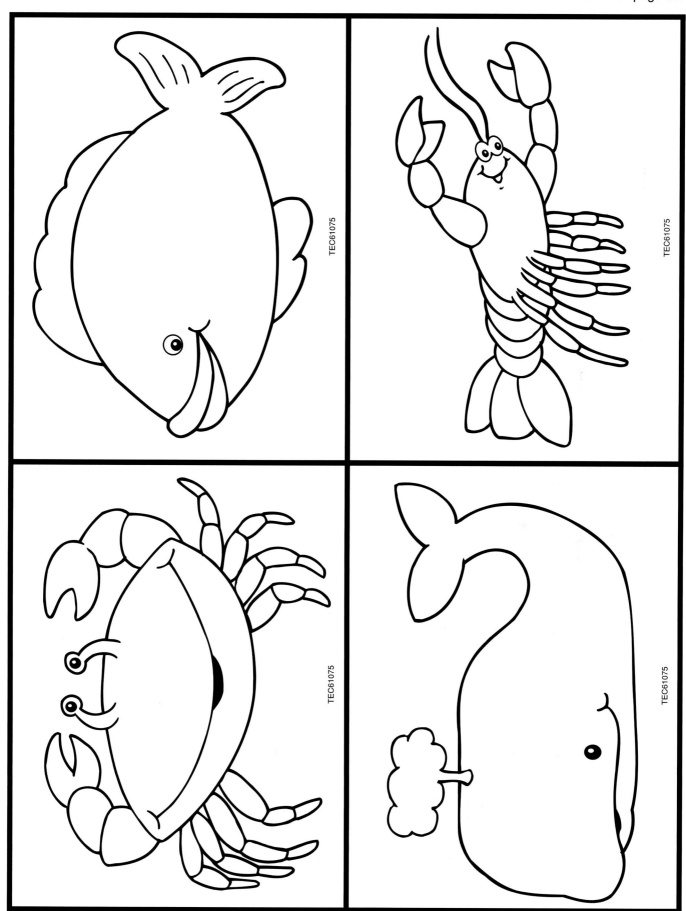

TEC61075

TEC61075

TEC61075

TEC61075

Sea Picture Cards

Use with "All Around the Sea" on page 86.

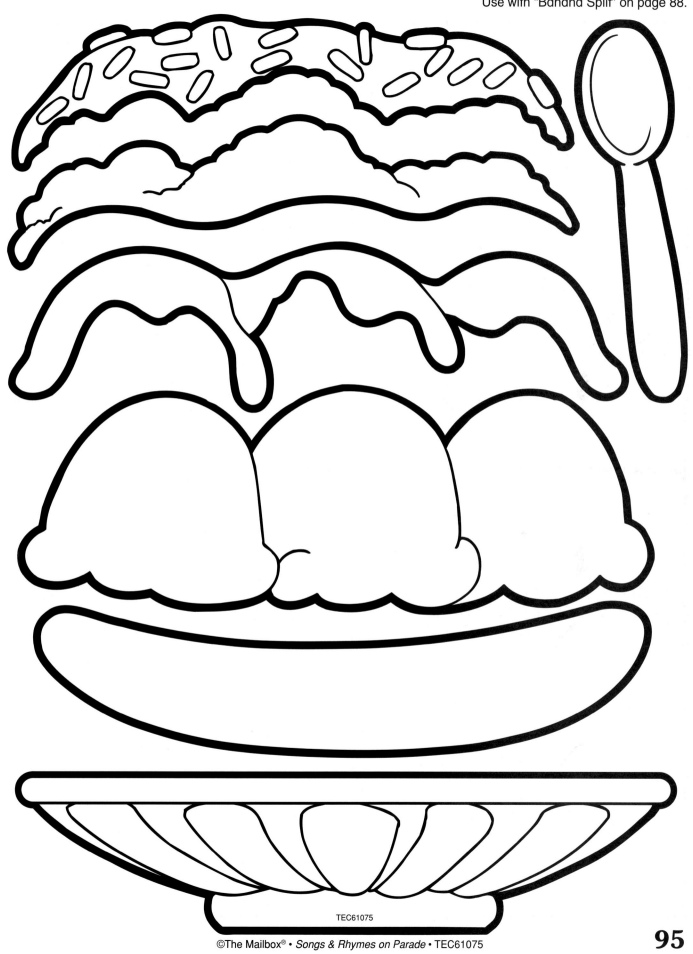

TEC61075

Summer Booklet

Use with "Watermelon Treat" on page 90.

1

Watermelon on the vine,

3

On the outside green and round,

Watermelon Treat

Name _____

2

Watermelon tastes so fine!

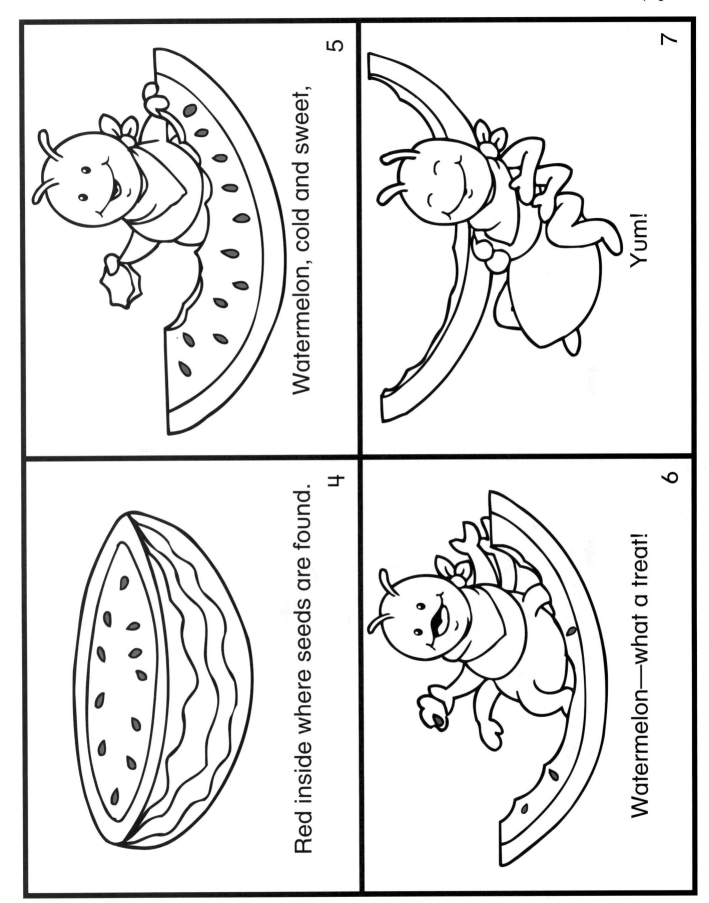

5

Watermelon, cold and sweet,

7

Yum!

4

Red inside where seeds are found.

6

Watermelon—what a treat!

Anytime

Welcome to Preschool

(sung to the tune of "Down by the Station")

Welcome to preschool! We're so glad to meet you.
We will read and sing to learn and make new friends.
We will count the numbers,
And we'll look at colors.
Let's go have fun
In preschool!

Try this:
- After singing the song, invite youngsters to settle in for a read-aloud of *Mouse's First Day of School* by Lauren Thompson. Then lead students in comparing the preschool activities in the song and in the story.

It's a School Day

(sung to the tune of "The Farmer in the Dell")

Oh, it's a school day.
Yes, it's a school day.
Hip hip
Hooray, hooray!
Yes, it's a school day.

Try this:
- Help your students learn the names of the days of the week by singing the name of the day instead of the phrase *school day*.

- Reinforce letter names by replacing *a school day* with *the letter* [b].

Celebrating Days

(sung to the tune of "Are You Sleeping?")

Can you name the
Days of the week?
Here we go!
Here we go!
Sunday, Monday, Tuesday,
Wednesday, Thursday, Friday,
Saturday.
Hip hooray!

Try this:
- Encourage youngsters to hop when they sing the current day's name.

- Divide youngsters into seven groups. Assign each group a different day's name to sing during the song. Then lead youngsters in singing several rounds, pointing to the corresponding groups during the fifth, sixth, and seventh lines.

Good Morning

(sung to the tune of "Bingo")

Let's say hello to all our friends!
Oh, won't you say, "Good morning?"
Good morning to you.
Good morning to you.
Good morning to you.
Oh, let's all say, "Good morning!"

Try this:
- While singing the song, have all youngsters say good morning to you during the third line, the girls wave and sing the fourth line, and the boys wave and sing the fifth line.

Circle-Time Song

(sung to the tune of "The More We Get Together")

Oh, come join me in the circle,
The circle, the circle.
Oh, come join me in the circle,
And let's have some fun
With talking, with sharing,
With singing, with caring.
Oh, come join me in the circle,
And let's have some fun.

Listen Up!

(sung to the tune of "Hot Cross Buns")

Get ready.
Get ready.
Listen closely for directions.
Get ready.

Transition Songs

(sung to the tune of "Head and Shoulders")

Cleaning:
It is time to clean our room, clean our room.
It is time to clean our room; clean our room!
Pick up toys and put them all away.
It is time to clean our room for the day!

Snacktime:
It is time to eat our snack, eat our snack.
It is time to eat our snack, eat our snack!
Wash our hands and say thank you for this food.
It is time to eat our snack, yummy snack!

Lining up:
It is time to line up now, come along.
It is time to line up now, come along!
Stand in line oh so very quietly.
It is time to line up now, follow me!

Walking Here to There

(sung to the tune of "If You're Happy and You Know It")

When we're walking down the hall, quiet please! (Sh! sh!)
When we're walking down the hall, quiet please! (Sh! sh!)
So that we do not disturb, we must walk and not be heard.
When we're walking down the hall, quiet please! (Sh! sh!)

Clean-the-Room Songs

(sung to the tune of "Down by the Station")

Clean, clean our classroom.
Clean the room together.
When we clean the room
We put our things away.

Cleanup time is easy
When we help each other.
Come on. Clean up.
Here we go!

(sung to the tune of "Hot Cross Buns")

Clean the room.
Clean the room.
Everybody
Work together.
Clean the room.

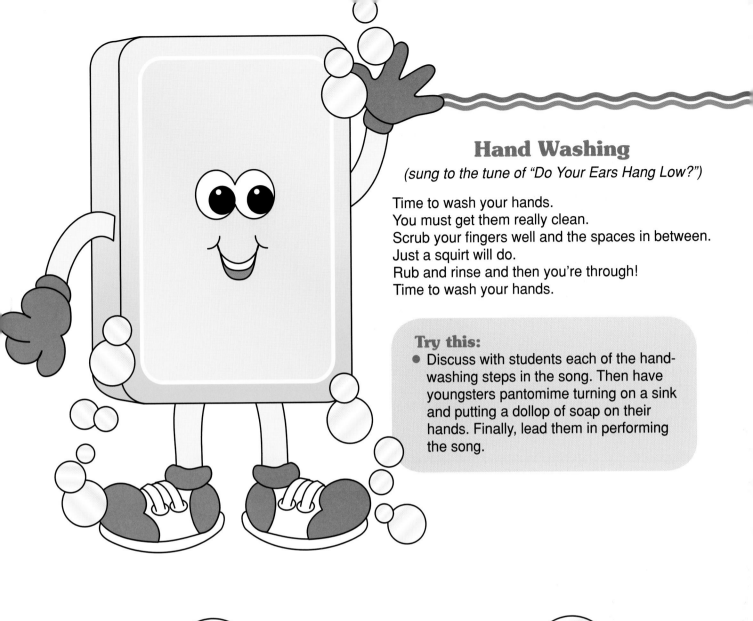

Hand Washing

(sung to the tune of "Do Your Ears Hang Low?")

Time to wash your hands.
You must get them really clean.
Scrub your fingers well and the spaces in between.
Just a squirt will do.
Rub and rinse and then you're through!
Time to wash your hands.

Try this:
● Discuss with students each of the hand-washing steps in the song. Then have youngsters pantomime turning on a sink and putting a dollop of soap on their hands. Finally, lead them in performing the song.

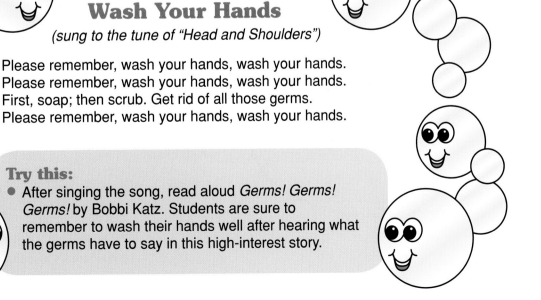

Wash Your Hands

(sung to the tune of "Head and Shoulders")

Please remember, wash your hands, wash your hands.
Please remember, wash your hands, wash your hands.
First, soap; then scrub. Get rid of all those germs.
Please remember, wash your hands, wash your hands.

Try this:
● After singing the song, read aloud *Germs! Germs! Germs!* by Bobbi Katz. Students are sure to remember to wash their hands well after hearing what the germs have to say in this high-interest story.

A Healthy Snack

(sung to the tune of "The Ants Go Marching")

A healthy snack is what we'll eat.
Hurrah! Hurrah!
A healthy snack, it can't be beat.
Hurrah! Hurrah!
A healthy snack is what we'll eat.
Please don't feed us anything sweet
For we want a healthy snack.
It is time; pass the treats,
Won't you please!

Try this:

● After singing the song, name a snack. If it is a healthy snack, encourage youngsters to cheer, "Hurrah! Hurrah!" If it is not, have them sit quietly. Continue in this manner with more snacks as time permits.

● Display the MyPyramid chart from the United States Department of Agriculture. Discuss with youngsters how fitness and good eating habits, as suggested in the song, contribute to a healthier lifestyle.

Please.

Thank you.

Good Manners

(sung to the tune of "Clementine")

Please and thank you
And you're welcome,
Mind your manners all the time.
Kindness spreads the more we share it.
Mind your manners; yes, that's fine!

Try this:

● Cut a large construction paper heart into a desired number of puzzle pieces. Each morning, sing the song as a reminder to use good manners. Then each time you hear a youngster say please, thank you, or you're welcome, post a puzzle piece on the bulletin board. When the heart is complete, celebrate youngsters' good manners with a special treat.

Ten.

I Can Count

(sung to the tune of "Are You Sleeping?")

Learning numbers,
Learning numbers,
One to ten,
One to ten.
I can count my fingers.
I can count my fingers,
One to ten,
One to ten.

(Have students count from one to ten on their fingers.)

Counting to 15!

(sung to the tune of "Mary Had a Little Lamb")

1, 2, 3, 4, 5, 6, 7,
8, 9, 10, and 11,
12 and 13, 14 too,
All the way to 15. Whew!

Try this:
● Have each youngster wipe his brow when he sings, "Whew!"

● Using the numbers 1 to 15, make a number card for each student. During a group singing of the song, have him hold up his card as he sings the corresponding number.

Three Shapes

Triangles have three sides.
Can you count them? 1, 2, 3.
Triangles have three sides.
Please count them again with me.

Squares have four sides.
Let's count them: 1, 2, 3, 4.
Squares have four sides.
Let's count again like before.

Circles have no sides,
Just as round as round can be.
Circles have no sides.
There are no points for you to see.

Try this:

● While reciting the rhyme, have each child use a finger to draw the corresponding shape on the floor, on a table, or in the air.

● Have groups of three and four youngsters lie on the floor to make human triangles and squares, respectively. Then chant the rhyme and count the sides of the corresponding human shapes.

The Shape Song

Provide shape cutouts for this song.

(sung to the tune of "If You're Happy and You Know It")

Put your [circle] in the air, in the air.
Put your [circle] in the air, in the air.
Put your [circle] in the air
And then wave it way up there.
Put your [circle] in the air, in the air.

Sing additional verses, substituting a different shape word each time.

Beautiful Colors

(sung to the tune of "For He's a Jolly Good Fellow")

Oh, [blue]'s a beautiful color.
Oh, [blue]'s a beautiful color.
Oh, [blue]'s a beautiful color.
It is like none other.

Sing additional verses, substituting a different color word each time.

Try this:

● Provide each child with a set of crayons. During each verse, have each child hold up the appropriate crayon.

● At the end of the song, invite a volunteer to name things in the room that match the featured color.

I've Been Learning All My Letters

(sung to the tune of "I've Been Working on the Railroad")

I've been learning all my letters
From *A* to letter *Z.*
I've been learning all my letters.
Listen up and you will see.
A, B, C, D, E, F, G, H,
I, J, K, L, M, N,
O, P, Q, R, S, T, U, V,
W, X, Y, Z.

Won't you sing with me?
Won't you sing with me?
Won't you sing the alphabet with me?
Won't you sing with me?
Won't you sing with me?
Oh, sing the alphabet with me!

Try this:

● Attach an alphabet strip to a paper headband for each student. Have her wear the headband while singing the song.

● Give each child a letter cutout or plastic letter. Have him hold up his letter at the appropriate time during the song.

Rhyming Song

(sung to the tune of "London Bridge")

Rhyming words is fun to do,
Fun to do, fun to do.
Rhyming words is fun to do—all together.

Name a word that rhymes with _____,
Rhymes with _____, rhymes with _____.
Name a word that rhymes with _____.
Let's all start now!

Try this:

● Ask a student volunteer to say a favorite word. Then lead the group in using the word to complete the phrases in the song. At the end of the song, help youngsters name both real and nonsense rhyming words.

● Share with youngsters a set of rhyming picture cards. Then put one card from each rhyming pair in a bag and post the rest of the cards for the group to see. Invite a child to remove a card from the bag, show it to the group, and name it. Then lead youngsters in singing the song, using the word to complete the phrases. At the end of the song, lead the class in naming the rhyming picture card.

A Story Follow-Up

(sung to the tune of "Oh Where, Oh Where Has My Little Dog Gone?")

What, oh what was the story about?
Oh what, oh what did we read?
Did it make you feel happy
Or make you feel mad?
Was it scary or funny or sad?

Left to Right
(sung to the tune of "Three Blind Mice")

Left to right,
Left to right,
That's how we read.
That's how we read.
Each word we read every day or night
Starts on the left and then goes to the right.
The words in our books are a beautiful sight!
Read left to right!

Try this:

● Write the song on chart paper. Then invite student volunteers, in turn, to use a pointer to track the words while the group sings the song.

● While singing, have youngsters demonstrate with a book the direction they should read.

The Reading Song
(sung to the tune of "The Farmer in the Dell")

[My teacher has a book], [my teacher has a book].
Hi, ho, it's good to know
[My teacher has a book].

Sing additional verses, replacing the underlined phrase with phrases such as *the book has a cover, the cover has a title, the words are on the page, the teacher reads out loud,* and *we'll listen to each word.*

Try this:

● Encourage each child to bring in a favorite book from the library or from home. Then invite her to share her book by substituting her name for the words *my teacher.*

Stars in the Sky

(sung to the tune of "The Itsy-Bitsy Spider")

See the shining stars
Up in the nighttime sky.
Can you see them twinkling
And blinking way up high?
When the morning comes,
The night turns into day
And the little twinkling stars
All seem to go away.

Try this:

- Use glitter glue to decorate one side of a star cutout (pattern on page 130). During the first four lines of the song, hold up the star with the glitter side facing the class. Then, during the remainder of the song, turn the star around so the glitter is no longer showing. Explain to youngsters that the star is still there but they can no longer see it shining.

- Make the room as dark as possible and shine a flashlight to represent a star. Then turn the classroom lights on to see how the light of the flashlight, like a star, fades into the other bright light. Then relate the last two lines of the song to the flashlight experience.

I float!

Sink or Float

(sung to the tune of "Head and Shoulders")

Will it sink or will it float, sink or float?
Will it sink or will it float, sink or float?
Will it sink to the bottom like a rock,
Or will it float just like a boat, sink or float?

Try this:

- Give each child a copy of a sink card and a float card from page 131. Hold up an object and lead youngsters in singing the song. At the end of the song, have each child predict whether the object will sink or float by holding up the corresponding card. Then place the item in water and discuss the results.

Day and Night
(sung to the tune of "Are You Sleeping?")

In the daytime, in the daytime,
You can see, you can see
Sunshine in the blue sky,
[Learning children], oh my,
All day long, all day long.

When it's nighttime, when it's nighttime,
You can see, you can see
Twinkling stars in moonlight,
[Owls swooping], what a sight,
All night long, all night long.

Sing additional verses, replacing the underlined phrases with corresponding phrases such as the following:
Day verses: *tapping builders, playing puppies, crawling babies*
Night verses: *raccoons eating, bats flying, fireflies blinking*

Try this:
- Give each child a cutout copy of the day and night cards on page 132. Have him hold up the corresponding card while singing the song.

- For each verse, hold up a day or night card (page 132) prior to singing and have youngsters act out the descriptive phrase.

Using Your Five Senses
(sung to the tune of "Clementine")

You are using
Your five senses
When you do these next five things:
Touching, seeing,
Tasting, hearing,
And then smelling anything.

Try this:
- For each child, accordion-fold a 4" x 24" strip of construction paper to create six boxes. Help each child glue to the strip a cutout copy of the five senses cards (page 133) in song order. Encourage youngsters to use the strips to help them sing the five senses song.

The Five Senses

"Sense-sational" Song
(sung to the tune of "The Farmer in the Dell")

We have five senses, yes!
We have five senses, yes!
Hi-ho, now did you know
We have five senses? Yes!

We have a sense of sight.
We have a sense of sight.
We use our eyes to see
Around us day and night.

We have a sense to hear.
We have a sense to hear.
We use our ears to hear
The sounds far and near.

We have a sense of smell.
We have a sense of smell.
We use our noses to sniff
The odors that we smell.

We have a sense of taste.
We have a sense of taste.
We use our mouths to taste
The foods we think are great!

We have a sense of touch.
We have a sense of touch.
We use our hands to touch
Things soft and rough and such.

Try this:
● Cut out a copy of the five senses cards on page 133. In turn, hold up each card and have youngsters identify the sense on the card and sing the corresponding verse.

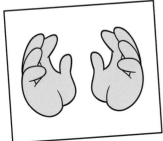

Five Senses
(sung to the tune of "Head and Shoulders")

My five senses help me learn, help me learn!
My five senses help me learn, help me learn!
My eyes, ears, nose, mouth, and hands all get a turn.
My five senses help me learn, help me learn!

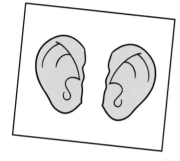

Weather With Action

What kind of weather will we have today
When we want to go out to play?

Will it be windy with lots of rain
Beating against the windowpane?

Or will there be snow swirling all around,
Making big fluffy piles on the ground?

We hope the sky is blue with a bright, warm sun,
For that kind of weather is the most fun!

Try this:
- Color and cut out a copy of the rainy, snowy, and sunny weather cards on page 134. Use the cards as visual clues to prompt youngsters while chanting the rhyme.

What's the Weather?

(sung to the tune of "Clementine")

What's the weather,
What's the weather,
What's the weather outside now?
Is it sunny? Is it snowing?
Is it raining outside now?

It is [sunny].
It is [sunny].
It is [sunny] outside now.
That's the weather we see today.
It is [sunny] outside now.

Try this:
- Write each line of the song on a separate sentence strip and place the strips in a pocket chart. Color and cut out four copies of the weather cards on page 134. Each day, invite a volunteer to look outside to determine the weather. Help him use the corresponding cards to complete each sentence. Then lead the group in singing the song!

Spring, Summer, Fall, and Winter

(sung to the tune of "Head and Shoulders")

Spring and summer, fall and winter, fall and winter!
Spring and summer, fall and winter, fall and winter!
Spring and summer, fall and winter too!
Spring and summer, fall and winter, fall and winter!

Try this:
- Give each child a copy of the four seasons cards on page 135. Have her point to the corresponding season as she sings.

Four Seasons Songs

(sung to the tune of "The Mulberry Bush")

First it is winter; then comes the spring.
A seasonal change brings summertime here.
Finally, comes the season of fall.
Four seasons in the whole year.

(sung to the tune of "The Muffin Man")

Oh, do you know the four seasons,
The four seasons, the four seasons?
Oh, do you know the four seasons?
We have four every year.

Winter, spring, summer, and fall,
Yes sirree, I know them all!
Winter, spring, summer, and fall,
The seasons of the year!

All Four Seasons

(sung to the tune of "Are You Sleeping?")

It is winter. It is winter.
See the snow. See the snow.
We can build a snowman. We can build a snowman.
It is cold! It is cold!

It is spring. It is spring.
See the rain. See the rain.
We see flowers growing. We see flowers growing.
The wind blows! The wind blows!

It is summer. It is summer.
It's so hot. It's so hot.
See the bright sun shining. See the bright sun shining.
Let's go swim! Let's go swim!

It is autumn. It is autumn.
See the leaves. See the leaves.
They're pretty, pretty colors, pretty, pretty colors.
Watch them fall! Watch them fall!

Try this:
- Color and cut out a copy of the four seasons cards on page 135. Hold up each card and have students identify each season. Then lead youngsters in singing the song, displaying each card as its corresponding verse is sung.

bus driver

Community Helpers
(sung to the tune of "Where Is Thumbkin?")

Where is firefighter?
Where is firefighter?
At the station,
At the station,
Ready to fight fires,
Ready to fight fires,
And keep us safe,
And keep us safe.

Continue with these lines:
Where is doctor? At the hospital, ready to bandage us, and make us well.
Where is police officer? At the station, ready to fight crime, and keep us safe.
Where is librarian? At the library, ready to read to us, and find us books.
Where is mail carrier? At the post office, ready to sort mail, to bring to us.
Where is teacher? At the school, ready to teach us lots, and care for us.
Where is pilot? At the airport, ready to fly the plane, and take us places.
Where is farmer? At the farm, ready to plant crops, to give us food.
Where is tailor? At his shop, ready to hem pants, and sew us clothes.
Where is waitress? At the restaurant, ready to take orders, and serve us food.
Where is builder? At the house, ready to hammer nails, and build the house.
Where is bus driver? On the road, ready to drive the bus, and take us home.

farmer

Try this:
● Color and cut out a copy of the community helper cards on pages 136 and 137. Hold up each card and have students identify each helper. Then lead youngsters in singing the song, displaying each card during its corresponding verse.

firefighter

pilot

police officer

Transportation

(sung to the tune of "Row, Row, Row Your Boat")

Go, go on a trip!
Do you have a plan?
Ship, plane, truck, or train?
Get there how you can!

Try this:

● Discuss the different sounds each mode of transportation makes. If desired, read an interactive read-aloud, such as *All Aboard: A True Train Story* by Susan Kuklin, and chant the many sounds of a train. Then gather youngsters to sing again, this time asking a volunteer to replace the third line with the sounds of his desired mode of transportation. When the song ends, ask youngsters to identify his travel selection.

Come Back, Teacher!

(sung to the tune of "My Bonnie Lies Over the Ocean")

[My teacher]'s been taken by aliens.
[My teacher] is in outer space.
[My teacher] is riding a spaceship.
Oh, bring back [my teacher] to me.

Bring back, bring back,
Oh, bring back [my teacher] to me, to me.
Bring back, bring back,
Oh, bring back [my teacher] to me.

For additional verses, replace "my teacher" with student names.

Try this:

● Replace "my teacher" with the name of another teacher and sing the song several times. Then discuss how the school would be different if the teacher brought back a few friendly aliens for each classroom!

First-Rate Family

(sung to the tune of "The Hokey-Pokey")

I love my family.
It is so good to me.
I love my family.
Yes, my family is great.
I feel so safe and happy
When I'm with my family.
My family's first rate!

Try this:
● Have each youngster draw a picture of her family. Label the picture "My Family" and have her point to the words each time she hears them in the song.

My Family

(sung to the tune of "Do Your Ears Hang Low?")

My whole family is the best that it can be.
I love everyone,
And I know that they love me.
They help me each day.
They love me in every way.
They're my family.

New Friendships
(sung to the tune of "She'll Be Comin' Round the Mountain")

It is fun to form new friendships every day.
We can make a lot of friends along the way.
We'll build friendships with each other.
We'll build friendships with another.
It is fun to form new friendships every day!

Try this:
- Lead students in singing the song each morning. Then when you see a youngster performing a friendly act during the day, present him with a Friendship Award (pattern on page 138).

- Have students stand in two straight parallel lines. As you lead youngsters in singing the song, have the first child in each line link arms and skip down the middle of the two lines together. Continue singing the song until each child has had a turn to skip with a partner.

- After singing the song several times, have youngsters share ways they can be kind to one another to build friendships.

Buddy Building
(sung to the tune of "This Land Is Your Land")

Your friends are my friends.
My friends are your friends.
We play together, learning from each other.
From a different country or a house next door—
Friendships keep growing day by day.

Try this:
- Encourage students to stand in a circle and join hands as they sing the song.

Helping Hands

(sung to the tune of "If You're Happy and You Know It")

If you see some friends in need, help them out.
If you see some friends in need, help them out.
If you see some friends in need, then you should help them out indeed.
If you see some friends in need, help them out.

Try this:
- Reward a little one for helping a friend in need by giving her a Friendship Award (pattern on page 138).

- Pair youngsters and have one sit on the floor as the other child stands. Have the child standing extend a hand to his partner during the first line of the song and the other hand during the second line. During the next two lines, have him help his friend stand. Then encourage youngsters to switch roles and sing again!

Sharing Is Fun

(sung to the tune of "Twinkle, Twinkle, Little Star")

Sharing is a lot of fun.
We can share with everyone.
Sharing books and new toys too
Helps me make new friends like you.
Sharing is a lot of fun.
Let's all share with everyone.

Try this:
- Repeat the third and fourth lines in the song to discuss how sharing books can build friendships. Then designate a time for youngsters to share a favorite book with a buddy.

School Lessons

(sung to the tune of "The Farmer in the Dell")

In school, I [learn to write].
In school, I [learn to write].
When I go, oh, don't you know,
In school, I [learn to write].

For additional verses, replace the underlined phrases with phrases such as the following:

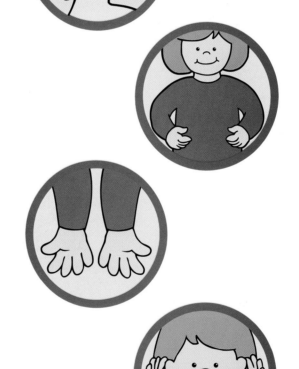

learn to count

learn to read

learn to share

listen well

Special Little Me!

(sung to the tune of "Twinkle, Twinkle, Little Star")

Special, special, little me!
No one is the same you see!
My own looks
And my own ways,
My own things to do each day.
Special, special, little me!
No one is the same you see!

Do You Know What I Can Do?

(sung to the tune of "The Muffin Man")

Oh, do you know what I can do,
What I can do,
What I can do?
Oh, do you know what I can do?
I can [jump on two feet]!

For additional verses, replace the underlined phrase
with phrases such as *clap with both hands, hop on
one foot, skip from side to side, snap my fingers,
shake my body,* and *wiggle all over.*

Try this:
● Lead youngsters in singing the song and
  encourage them to act out the last line. When
  they do, sing back to them, "Yes, I see what
  you can do, what you can do, what you can do!
  Yes, I see what you can do! You can [jump on
  two feet]!"

I'm a Special Kid

(sung to the tune of "Row, Row, Row Your Boat")

I'm a special kid.

Take a look at me!

I am smart and I'm a part

Of this whole class, you see.

Try this:
- Keep a sample of each student's outstanding work. Then gather youngsters and invite each child, in turn, to sing the song (with your help) and show off his wonderful work!

Get Moving!

(sung to the tune of "This Old Man")

I have feet; so do you.
Look at what my feet can do:
Run and walk and dance and hop, hop, hop.
Feet can move and never stop.

I have hands; so do you.
Look at what my hands can do:
Wave and shake and point and clap, clap, clap.
Hands can move and never stop.

I have a body; so do you.
Look at what my body can do:
Shake and wiggle and turn and drop, drop, drop.
Bodies can move and then must STOP!

Ways to Exercise

(sung to the tune of "The Mulberry Bush")

This is the way we [bend our knees],
[Bend our knees], [bend our knees].
This is the way we [bend our knees]
To exercise our bodies.

Sing additional verses, replacing the underlined phrase with phrases such as *jog in place, circle our arms, march in place,* and *touch our toes*.

Babies at the Farm

(sung to the tune of "She'll Be Comin' Round the Mountain")

There are baby [ducks] called [ducklings] at the farm. [Quack, quack!]
There are baby [ducks] called [ducklings] at the farm. [Quack, quack!]
There are baby [ducks] called [ducklings].
There are baby [ducks] called [ducklings].
There are baby [ducks] called [ducklings] at the farm. [Quack, quack!]

For additional verses, replace the underlined animals and animal sounds with other animals and sounds such as the following:
cows, calves, moo, moo
pigs, piglets, oink, oink
cats, kittens, meow, meow

Try this:
- Color and cut out a copy of the farm animal cards on pages 139 and 140. Prior to singing each verse, hold up the corresponding card and have students name the animal.

Six Little Pigs

(sung to the tune of "Six Little Ducks")

Six little [pigs] that I once knew,
Fat ones, skinny ones, [pink] ones too.
But the one little [pig] with the [curl] in his tail,
He led the others with a(n) [oink, oink, oink],
[Oink, oink, oink, oink, oink, oink].
He led the others with a(n) [oink, oink, oink].

For additional verses, replace the underlined words and animal sounds with other words and sounds such as the following:
cows, brown, cow, swish, moo
chicks, yellow, chick, feather, cluck
sheep, white, sheep, wool, baa
ducks, yellow, duck, fluff, quack

Try this:
- Color and cut out a copy of the pig, cow, hen, duck, and sheep animal cards on pages 139 and 140. Glue each card to a craft stick to make a puppet. Once students are familiar with the song, invite six youngsters to stand in a line and give the first person a puppet. Encourage her to lead her classmates around the room as they sing and act out the first verse. Then invite other students to act out the remaining verses in the same manner.

Moo!

Sounds at the Farm

(sung to the tune of "Did You Ever See a Lassie?")

Have you ever heard a [cow], a [cow], a [cow]?
Have you ever heard a [cow] say [moo, moo, moo, moo]?
[Moo, moo, moo, moo, moo, moo, moo, moo, moo, moo, moo, moo].
Have you ever heard a [cow] say [moo, moo, moo, moo]?

For additional verses, replace the underlined animals and animal sounds with other animals and sounds, such as the following: *duck (quack), pig (oink), horse (neigh), sheep (baa), dog (woof), cat (meow),* and *chicken (cluck).*

Try this:

● Once students are familiar with the song, give each child a copy of one of the farm animal cards on pages 139 and 140. For each verse, have the youngsters holding the corresponding animal cards sing the third line.

● Divide your class into two groups and ask them to pretend that they are animals talking to each other. During the third line of the song, have one group sing three "moos" and then the other group sing three "moos" and repeat! Continue with additional verses.

Dinosaurs Stomping

(sung to the tune of "The Ants Go Marching")

Dinos stomping [one by one].
Let's stomp! Let's stomp!
Dinos stomping [one by one].
Let's stomp! Let's stomp!
Dinos stomping [one by one].
The little one stomped [to have some fun].   [*(Hands over head cheering.)*]
And they all went stomping down
On the ground
To see how it sounds!   *(Hands over ears.)*
Boom! Boom! Boom!

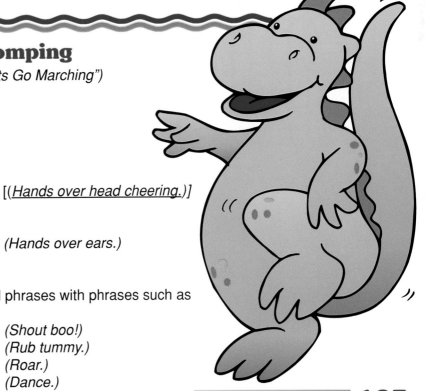

For additional verses, replace the underlined phrases with phrases such as the following:

Two by two; and hollered, "Boo!"   *(Shout boo!)*
Three by three; and ate a tree!   *(Rub tummy.)*
Four by four; and gave a roar!   *(Roar.)*
Five by five; and danced the jive!   *(Dance.)*

Zoo Sounds

(sung to the tune of "The Wheels on the Bus")

The [bear] in the zoo goes [grrrr, grrrr, grrrr],
[Grrrr, grrrr, grrrr, grrrr, grrrr, grrrr].
The [bear] in the zoo goes [grrrr, grrrr, grrrr]
All through the day.

For additional verses, replace the animal name
and sound with other zoo animals and their
corresponding sounds.

Try this:
- Give each child an animal-shaped plate.
  Have students sit in groups based on
  their plates. Then lead students in singing
  verses to correspond with their critters.

Have You Been to the Zoo?

(sung to the tune of "The Muffin Man")

Oh, have you been to see the zoo,
To see the zoo, to see the zoo?
Oh, have you been to see the zoo,
To see the [orange tigers]?

For additional verses, replace the underlined
phrase with other phrases such as *tan lions, brown
bears, striped zebras,* and *pretty penguins.*

Try this:
- Program a sheet of chart paper with the
  phrase "*When I go to the zoo, I want to see
  the* _____." Invite
  volunteers, in turn, to complete the phrase.
  Use each response to lead youngsters in
  singing a new verse of the song.

Oh, I Love the Circus

(sung to the tune of "Pop! Goes the Weasel")

All around the big circus tent
The funny clowns all run by.
The acrobats are swinging high.
I love the circus!

All around the big circus tent
The animals all march by.
The tightrope walkers balance high.
Oh, I love the circus!

Try this:

● Attach a long strip of masking tape to the floor to represent a tightrope.
Invite student volunteers to walk forward, backward, or sideways on
the high wire while their classmates sing the song.

● Assemble student copies of the booklet on pages 141 and 142. Have
each child complete her booklet by writing her name and coloring the
illustrations. Then help her use her booklet as a prop to sing the first
verse of the song.

Oh, Circus Clown

(sung to the tune of "O Christmas Tree")

Oh, circus clown, oh circus clown,
You always keep me smiling.
Oh, circus clown, oh circus clown,
You always keep me smiling.
You make me grin without a sound.
You make me laugh when I am down.
Oh, circus clown, oh circus clown,
You always keep me smiling.

Try this:

● Have each youngster color a copy of a clown cutout (pattern on
page 142). Then lead students in singing to their happy clowns.

● Invite youngsters to suggest things a clown might do in a circus
act to make the audience smile. Then encourage little ones to
act out each suggested clown performance during the song.

● Give each child a clown cutout (pattern on page 142). Challenge
youngsters to hold up their clowns each time they hear the word
clown in the song.

Star Pattern
Use with "Stars in the Sky" on page 110.

TEC61075

Sink 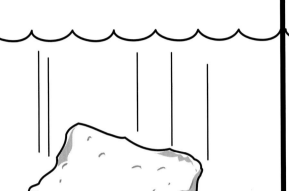 TEC61075	Float TEC61075
Sink 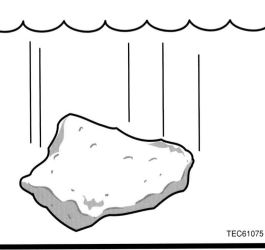 TEC61075	Float TEC61075

Day and Night Cards

Use with "Day and Night" on page 111.

TEC61075

Use with "Using Your Five Senses" on page 111 and "'Sense-sational' Song" on page 112.

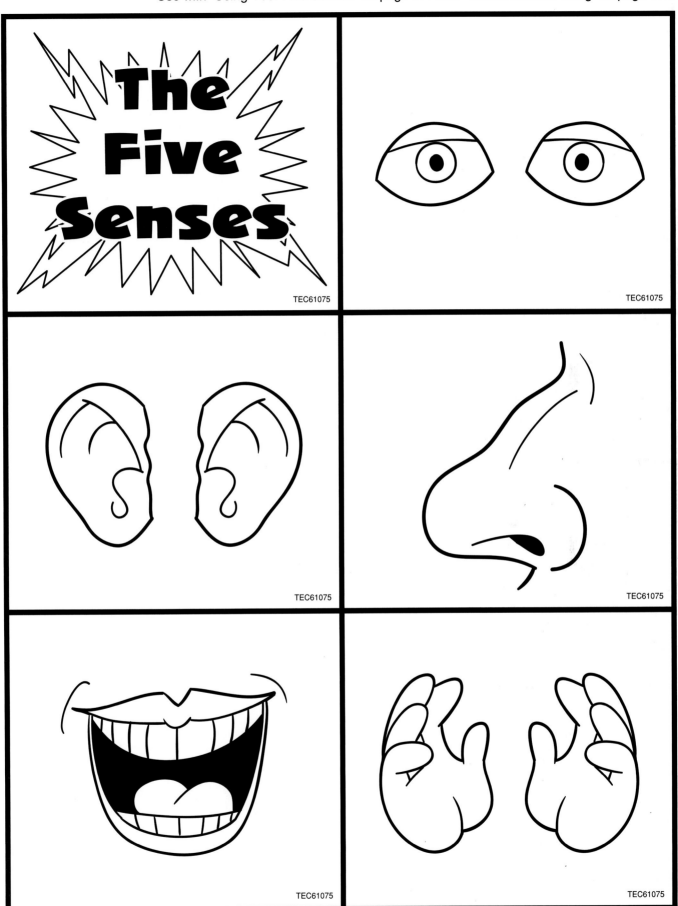

TEC61075

TEC61075

TEC61075

TEC61075

TEC61075

TEC61075

Weather Cards

Use with "Weather With Action" on page 113 and "What's the Weather?" on page 114.

sunny
TEC61075

snowy
TEC61075

rainy
TEC61075

windy
TEC61075

foggy
TEC61075

cloudy
TEC61075

Use with "Spring, Summer, Fall, and Winter" on page 114 and "All Four Seasons" on page 116.

Friendship Awards
Use with "New Friendships" on page 120 and "Helping Hands" on page 121.

FRIENDSHIP AWARD

_____
student

Thank you for your kindness!

_____
teacher

FRIENDSHIP AWARD

_____
student

Thank you for your kindness!

_____
teacher

Farm Animal Cards

Use with "Babies at the Farm" and "Six Little Pigs" on page 126 and "Sounds at the Farm" on page 127.

Farm Animal Cards

Use with "Babies at the Farm" and "Six Little Pigs" on page 126 and "Sounds at the Farm" on page 127.

TEC61075

TEC61075

TEC61075

TEC61075

All around the big circus tent

1

The acrobats are swinging high.

3

I LOVE THE CIRCUS

ADMIT ONE

Name _____

©The Mailbox® • Songs & Rhymes on Parade • TEC61075

The funny clowns all run by.

2

Anytime Booklet
Use with "Oh, I Love the Circus" on page 129.

I love the circus!

4

Clown Pattern
Use with "Oh, Circus Clown" on page 129.

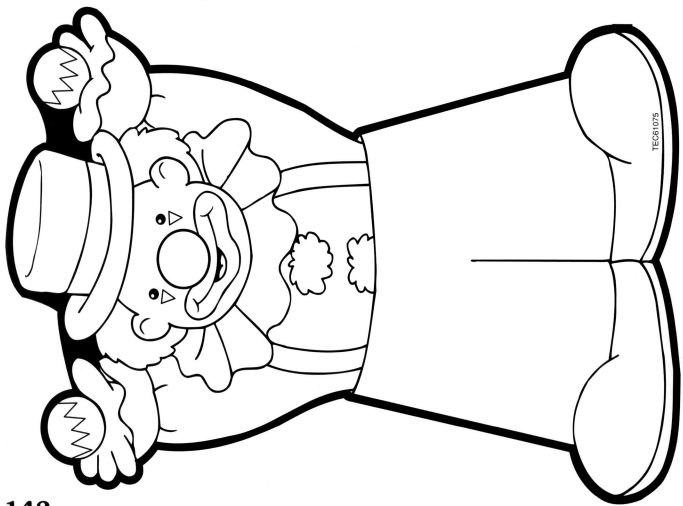

142

Index